GLASNOST, PERESTROIKA, AND U.S. DEFENSE SPENDING

Studies in Defense Policy

SELECTED TITLES

GLASNOST, PERESTROIKA, AND U.S. DEFENSE SPENDING

William W. Kaufmann

THE BROOKINGS INSTITUTION
Washington, D.C.

FOREWORD

THE Bush administration has now made it clear that it wants President Mikhail S. Gorbachev to succeed in his efforts to institute major economic and political reforms in the Soviet Union and Eastern Europe. With strong encouragement from Moscow, it has also engaged its allies and the Warsaw Pact in negotiations for a balanced reduction of nuclear and conventional arms and is proceeding toward an agreement with the USSR on a cut in strategic nuclear forces. At the same time, the administration has reversed its position on spending for national defense. Only eight months ago, President Bush proposed a plan calling for an average annual increase (after inflation) of 1.7 percent between fiscal years 1990 and 1994. Now, in December of 1989, Secretary of Defense Richard Cheney is considering reductions that could amount to as much as $195 billion between fiscal 1991 and 1995.

Despite these dramatic changes, major questions remain about the direction in which U.S. defense policy should be headed during the coming decade. For example, what cuts can be made even before any formal agreements are concluded with the Soviet Union? Should the United States seek arms reductions beyond those already under negotiation? How, if at all, should it revise the assumptions on which to base the planning of its forces? And what shape might these forces take by the end of the century?

In this study William W. Kaufmann starts from the premise that the United States has a large stake in ending the cold war, minimizing the military competition, and furthering economic and political change in the Soviet bloc. Consequently, he suggests that both the Soviet Union and the United States, whether by mutual understanding or by treaty, continue to transfer resources from military to civilian purposes even if the process lasts no more than a decade and even if Gorbachev falls from power. He points out in this connection that real U.S. spending for national defense has already declined by more than 6 percent since 1987 and that, even in the absence of any new treaties, it could be reduced by another 13 percent without jeopardizing current U.S. capabilities and commitments. Subsequent agreements with the Soviet Union and the Warsaw Pact, dealing with the whole range of military capabilities on both sides, could eventually lower U.S. real national defense spending to $160 billion by the end of the decade.

Within this constraint, according to Kaufmann, the United States could still maintain a powerful and flexible nuclear deterrent. It could also retain substantial active-duty and reserve forces for the defense of Europe as well as for several lesser contingencies such as might arise in the Middle East and other volatile but important areas of the world.

William Kaufmann is a nonresident senior fellow of the Brookings Foreign Policy Studies program and a member of the faculty of the John F. Kennedy School of Government at Harvard University. He is grateful to Robert Howard, Franklin Lindsay, John D. Steinbruner, and Richard Stubbing for their comments on the manuscript. Caroline Lalire edited the manuscript, and Vernon L. Kelley verified its factual content. Ann M. Ziegler typed the text and tables, Susan Woollen prepared it for typesetting, and Charlotte B. Brady and Susan A. Stewart provided administrative assistance.

Brookings is grateful for funding provided for this study by the John D. and Catherine T. MacArthur Foundation and the Carnegie Corporation of New York.

The views expressed in the study are those of the author and should not be ascribed to persons or organizations whose assistance is acknowledged, or to the trustees, officers, or staff members of the Brookings Institution.

BRUCE K. MAC LAURY
President

December 1989
Washington, D.C.

CONTENTS

TABLES

Tables begin on page 55

GLASNOST, PERESTROIKA, AND
U.S. DEFENSE SPENDING

CHAPTER ONE

THE ISSUE OF REDUCED DEFENSE SPENDING

MIKHAIL S. GORBACHEV'S rise to the summit of the Soviet government and the changes he has instituted in the communist bloc and international relations since 1986 raise an urgent question. To what extent should the United States alter its defense establishment, programs, and budgets during the last decade of the twentieth century? The Bush administration proposes to spend nearly $300 billion on national defense in fiscal 1990,[1] and both the executive branch and, until recently, a majority of Congress seem to take that amount as a fact of life and as appropriate to existing international conditions. From a somewhat different perspective, however, such a commitment of national resources might be seen as the abnormal result of some quite abnormal circumstances that, if altered, would produce substantial reductions in defense spending.

Trends in U.S. Defense Spending

After all, it was only a little more than fifty years ago that U.S. defense spending amounted to $14 billion (in 1990 dollars) and took less than 2 percent of the nation's gross national product (see table 1).[2] Even in the wake of World War II, with all the new international responsibilities thrust upon the United States, national defense spending between 1947 and 1950 averaged approximately $101 billion a year, admittedly influenced in part by the American monopoly of atomic weapons. Only after the U.S. vision of a cooperative world order under the aegis of the United Nations fell victim to Stalin's subjugation of Eastern Europe, his attempts to subvert

1. All subsequent references to years for U.S. defense programs are fiscal years.
2. All subsequent dollar amounts are in 1990 dollars unless otherwise indicated.

the democracies of Western Europe, the Soviet blockade of West Berlin, the seizure of power in China by Mao Tse-tung, and the outbreak of the Korean War did American policy shift fully from cooperation to containment. By 1949 the United States had become a founding member of the North Atlantic Treaty Organization (NATO). The war in Korea hardened the American view of the Soviet Union as an expansionist power, led to a rapid growth in U.S. security commitments to Asia, and began an era of large increases in the defense budget.

The growth in spending was uneven. President Dwight D. Eisenhower tried to bring the defense budget down after the truce in Korea, but it still remained more than twice as high as it had been before the war, in large part because of the expansion of U.S. nuclear capabilities. After further increases and decreases under Presidents Kennedy, Johnson, Nixon, Ford, and Carter, President Ronald Reagan gave an upward impetus to defense spending that was unprecedented in American peacetime history. Between 1980 and 1990, outlays for national defense grew in real terms by nearly 35 percent. Between 1950 (before the North Korean attack) and 1990, those same outlays expanded by a factor of nearly three—from approximately $106 billion to $300 billion—even as they declined as a percent of a growing GNP (table 1).

The trend in Soviet defense expenditures is much more difficult not only to ascertain but also to equate in comparable terms with what has happened in the United States. However, use of the dollar-costing methodology of the CIA (which calculates the price of buying the Soviet military establishment in the U.S. economy) suggests that the two countries started from about the same spending base after World War II. During the 1950s and 1960s, however, the United States appears to have outspent the Soviet Union, largely because of the defense cutbacks made by General Secretary Nikita S. Khrushchev. With the advent of Leonid I. Brezhnev, this policy was reversed, and Soviet outlays began to average an annual real growth of approximately 3 percent until the mid-1970s. Since then, real growth has been 2 percent or less a year and, according to Gorbachev, has not grown at all since 1987 (see table 2). Nonetheless, it would appear that the two countries were on about equal terms in defense spending by the end of the 1980s, although defense as a share of the Soviet GNP was probably at least three times higher than the comparable share of defense in the United States. In other words, if both sides roughly tripled their defense spending during the last forty years, the burden fell much more painfully on the Soviet Union than on the United States in its consumption of resources in general and modern technology in particular.

The Current Situation

Despite these expenditures—or perhaps because of them—the two principal spheres of influence (with one major exception) remained remarkably stable regardless of frequent forecasts of an imminent Soviet breakout in Europe, Africa, the Middle East, Southwest Asia, and even Latin America. The one great exception, of course, was the departure of China, not from communist dictatorship but from the communist bloc. Elsewhere, whatever changes occurred, their significance proved more symbolic than substantive.

Whether Khrushchev, had he remained in power, would or could have ended the military competition and removed its underlying causes remains uncertain. What does seem clear is that Gorbachev is moving well beyond what Khrushchev had begun to attempt. At a minimum, Gorbachev appears to be looking for a long respite from the cold war. More optimistically (and quite conceivably), he is seeking, among other goals, to reform the political and economic systems of the Soviet Union, to end the cold war and the military competition, and to shift resources from the military sector to the civilian economy. As evidence of his sincerity, he has withdrawn Soviet forces from Afghanistan and encouraged settlement of the conflicts in Namibia, Angola, and Cambodia. There is even hope that he will reduce Soviet subsidies to Cuba and Nicaragua. Somewhat to the consternation of the industrial democracies he has asked to become included in their deliberations.

Equally important, Gorbachev has tried through both unilateral and collaborative measures to emphasize that the Soviet Union is more interested in military stability between the major alliances at reduced cost than in military advantages, offensive action and preemption, and a heavy-handed control over countries bordering on the Soviet Union. He is obviously eager to continue the strategic arms reduction talks (START); to the surprise of its American sponsors, he agreed to the "double zero" of the Intermediate-Range Nuclear Forces (INF) Treaty, which eliminated all ballistic missiles in the ranges of 300 to 3,300 miles, even though he gave up approximately six warheads for every one the NATO allies ceded;

he has offered to negotiate the destruction of all short-range nuclear missiles in Europe and has proposed unilateral cuts of 500 nuclear weapons once the negotiations begin; and perhaps most astonishing of all, he has announced a cut of 500,000 in the Soviet armed forces and agreed to the establishment of conventional parity between NATO and the Warsaw Pact in the area of the Atlantic to the Urals, even though, once again, that will require the Pact to give up more personnel and weapons than NATO. Beyond all that, Gorbachev has announced that Soviet military doctrine would be reoriented toward defensive operations, told the East European nations to choose their own paths to socialism, and seemingly repudiated the Brezhnev doctrine, which declared the right of the Soviet Union to intervene militarily to uphold communist rule in Eastern Europe.

One can certainly argue about Gorbachev's long-term motives in unleashing this torrent of proposals, actions, and reactions. One can also insist that the Soviet Union show greater movement toward human rights and democracy before the United States and its allies engage in far-reaching modifications of their current military capabilities. But it is worth remembering as well that Gorbachev seems to be offering a respite from the cold war that could last at least a generation and that the United States also has incentives to reduce the military confrontation and competition even if they should resume at a later date. It is not as if America lacked economic problems of its own, although there are many ways to solve them without any changes in programmed defense spending. Nonetheless, reductions in defense—if justifiable on military grounds—would offer some help in meeting a number of social and economic demands, however unlikely it is that feasible reductions would make all problems disappear.

Choices

The United States could obviously afford larger defense budgets, provided that sacrifices were made elsewhere. But we must recognize that to have high confidence of achieving deterrence and stability at both nuclear and conventional levels, given Soviet military capabilities, would cost a good deal more than we and our allies are now spending. Thus, at a time when there is great pressure to reduce the federal budget deficit, and even greater resistance to any increase in federal taxes, policymakers in the executive branch and Congress have a choice. They can seek a formidable deterrent, and pay the price with defense budgets that increase in real terms by as much as 7 percent a year—as the Reagan administration tried to do—with reasonable confidence that the Soviets will follow suit, however great the pain. Or they can take the path staked out to a considerable degree by Ronald Reagan as well as Mikhail Gorbachev.

Certainly the latter choice is the more efficient one. The two sides may differ about what constitutes stability and what forces, readiness, and rates of modernization are necessary to its maintenance. But it would appear to be cheaper to reduce forces to an agreed level of stability than to increase them competitively without any accepted definition of what constitutes a stable military situation. Furthermore, for what it is worth, the first rather than the second course now commands the most public support. Although in a recent poll 60 percent of the respondents continued to approve of keeping U.S. troops in Europe, two-thirds of them believed that Moscow was no longer an immediate threat, and 75 percent considered nuclear war unlikely.[3] That is not a mandate for increased defense.

In short, there is much to be said for seeking military stability through arms reductions and savings in defense outlays. But how to get from here to there, wherever there may turn out to be, is bound to be more complex. Essentially, two different ways suggest themselves. The first, in the great British tradition now becoming thoroughly Americanized, is to muddle through from one year to the next, without any clearly defined operational goals or programs. In fact, it is not unfair to say that this is the path down which the executive branch and Congress have embarked. For all practical purposes it has meant negotiating in the various arms control arenas with one hand and proposing increased defense spending with the other (see table 3). It has also meant an annual ritual of congressional cuts in outlays largely determined by the deficit targets of Gramm-Rudman-Hollings and a variety of parochial interests, even though defense spending has actually declined very little from its peak of fiscal 1987 (table 1).[4] One consequence of this peculiar process is that no one considers how defense planning and budgeting should interact with arms reduction negotiations in Geneva and

3. Times-CBS poll of May 11, 1989, reported in *New York Times*, May 29, 1989, p. A6.
4. Gramm-Rudman-Hollings refers to the Balanced Budget and Emergency Control Act of 1985 (P.L. 99-177) as amended by the Balanced Budget and Emergency Deficit Control Reaffirmation Act of 1987 (P.L. 100-119).

Vienna to help them along.[5] Another consequence is that the president cannot point with pride to the pattern of defense restraint (at least in the appropriation of new budget authority) that has lasted now for five years. Nor can he stress that, while Gorbachev is talking about reductions in Soviet defense spending, the United States has already begun to make its own.

The Process of Change

Fortunately there is another way to proceed. It is to recognize that the process of reversing the military buildup while increasing stability along the way—if it is to occur at all—is likely to go forward in stages over a period of as much as a decade.

President George Bush has already expressed the hope that the negotiations on conventional arms reductions can be completed in a year or less, and some negotiators claim that 95 percent of the strategic arms reduction treaty is finished. But the issues still to be faced in Vienna and Geneva remain so complex that four or five more years may be needed to resolve them and carry out the agreed reductions. In the circumstances it would be prudent to anticipate a first stage of the process during which both sides clarify their objectives and proposals and make sure that their defense programs do not place obstacles in the way of arms reductions and stability, yet (at least in the United States) take out military insurance against a breakdown of the process. A second stage that would almost certainly take several years would entail adjustment of NATO and Warsaw Pact forces to the terms of the nuclear and conventional arms agreements, with due regard for stability, cost, and future modernization. Finally, assuming these two stages were successfully negotiated, a third stage could well follow. In a period of three or four years, during which a further reduction in nuclear forces might be obtained, conventional forces outside the area of the Atlantic to the Urals, including naval forces, would be brought within the control regime, and—with a substantial diminution of any immediate threat from the Soviet Union—U.S. planners would have

---

5. The START negotiations in Geneva have as their goal a reduction of 50 percent in strategic nuclear warheads. The CFE (conventional forces in Europe) negotiations in Vienna seek to establish parity in conventional arms between NATO and the Warsaw Pact in the area between the Atlantic and the Urals.

to engage in a major redesign of American military objectives, forces, and defense budgets.

To describe the process of unwinding the military coils of the cold war is all well and good. But how, specifically, might each of the three successive stages in the process affect U.S. defense capabilities and spending? How should the Pentagon prepare for changes not only in force size and composition but also in deployments, readiness, long-range mobility, sustainability (through war reserve stocks), and modernization, with all its implications for the defense-industrial base?

CHAPTER TWO

THE FIVE-YEAR DEFENSE PROGRAM, 1990–94

IT MAY BE tempting to believe that proposals for arms reductions, negotiations in Geneva and Vienna, and proposed increases in defense budget authority and spending constitute a coherent short-run response to the challenges ahead. However, pressures to reduce defense budget authority (and to a lesser extent outlays) have existed since early 1986. They are likely only to increase as the federal budget deficit remains well above the Gramm-Rudman-Hollings targets, as the list of domestic problems lengthens, and as the Soviet Union appears to become less and less of a military threat.

A Revised FYDP

It would seem logical, in the circumstances, for the Bush administration to revise its five-year defense program (FYDP) in two more or less simultaneous steps. During the first, it would make cuts, primarily in investments, so as to bring national defense outlays for 1990 to 1994 down from a total of $1,665.7 billion to $1,500 billion. Such a step would acknowledge the unreality of the FYDP that President Bush inherited by disposing of or deferring many programs that the Bush FYDP cannot seriously fund and, at the same time, cancel the personnel increases required to support those programs (more than 62,000 military personnel).

In the second step, national defense outlays between 1990 and 1994 would be reduced from a total of $1,500 billion to $1,413.3 billion as a result of changes in force structure, marked principally by reductions in strategic nuclear capabilities and aircraft carrier battle groups. Although cumulative savings from these two steps would theoretically amount to

$252.4 billion, realistically outlays would fall only from $300 billion to $265 billion, and the cumulative difference between the latest proposals by Secretary of Defense Richard B. Cheney and a reduced FYDP would come to $134.7 billion (see tables 3, 4, 5). Such a revision in defense programs would substitute a gradual decline in real national defense outlays for a relatively modest but unrealistic increase. At the same time it would halt the rush for new weapons at a time when arms reductions and military stability have become paramount U.S. objectives. Yet the revision would hedge (or take out insurance) against setbacks or failures during this delicate period of transition in the Soviet Union, Eastern Europe, and China.

President Bush and his advisers are certainly right to want to avoid lulling the United States and the allies into a false sense of security after only five years of experience with the new thinking of the Soviet Union. Fortunately, they are in a position to design a new FYDP that cuts defense spending and at the same time retains a more efficient military capability than we have now. Indeed, the overabundant legacy of the Reagan administration—reflected in the balances of prior-year defense budget authority (amounting to about $281 billion in current dollars)—permits them to have their cake and eat it too.[6]

Strategic Nuclear Forces

The strategic nuclear forces are in particular need of review, not only because they are a continuous source of controversy but also because the funds devoted to them nearly doubled from 1980 to 1988.[7] Spending for them in fiscal 1990 will amount to $52 billion (see table 7). This rapid increase in funding came about partly because of concerns about the "window of vulnerability," even though, after a devastating Soviet first strike and only tactical warning, the U.S. offensive capabilities already in place could probably have delivered more than 3,500 warheads on targets in the Soviet Union in retaliation.[8] Admittedly, the continuation

6. See table 6 for balances of prior-year budget authority, 1988 to 1990. According to the *Department of Defense Annual Report, Fiscal Year 1990*, p. 84, $110.1 billion in outlays for fiscal 1990 will result from these prior-year balances.

7. See *National Defense Budget Estimates for FY 1988–1989* (Office of the Assistant Secretary of Defense, Comptroller, May 1987), p. 77.

8. William W. Kaufmann, *A Reasonable Defense* (Brookings, 1986), p. 82.

of such a powerful deterrent required a program of modernization, and previous administrations had already put one in place. Its purpose was to shore up each leg of the strategic triad, consisting of land-based intercontinental ballistic missiles (ICBMs), long-range bombers, and submarine-launched ballistic missiles (SLBMs). The program was intended to permit the second-strike coverage of more than 4,000 targets in the Soviet Union, while allowing the president to limit the U.S. retaliation to some subset of the total target list, and to ensure that under no circumstances could the Soviet leadership conceive of gaining a meaningful advantage from a strategic exchange.

The Reagan Initiatives

Not content with this program and strategy, the Reagan administration revived the B-1 bomber and hastened it to deployment, continued development of the Stealth (B-2) bomber, upgraded the B-52 bombers yet again, pushed deployment of air-launched and sea-launched cruise missiles (ALCM and SLCM), added the small ICBM to the MX for land-based ballistic missile deployment, and continued deployment of Trident submarines along with development of the D-5 (Trident II) ballistic missile, which would have a prompt hard-target-kill capability approximating that of the land-based MX. It also set out to upgrade the surveillance, early warning, and communications network of the strategic nuclear forces and talked about the possibility of prevailing in a prolonged nuclear war.

Perhaps even more important, the Reagan administration attempted to improve the damage-limiting capabilities of the United States. It sought, unsuccessfully, to revive the large-scale civil defense program that had faltered and failed in the 1960s. It modernized and added to the early warning system against bombers. It also replaced a number of aging fighter-interceptors and launched what was to be a major air defense initiative. And to the surprise of many, President Reagan himself introduced the strategic defense initiative (SDI), an increasingly costly program that was supposed to make ballistic missiles impotent and obsolete.

It has been estimated that when the Pentagon assumed that real growth in the defense budget would average about 7 percent each year, the cost of these offensive and defensive investments would amount to approximately $178 billion (in 1989 dollars) between 1990 and 1994.[9] Since then,

---

9. Stephen Alexis Cain, *Strategic Forces Funding in the 1990s: A Renewed Buildup?* (Defense Budget Project, April 1989), pp. 13, 17, 18, 19. All totals are in 1989 dollars.

none of the programs—except for a large-scale civil defense—has been dropped. However, as defense budgets have declined, particular programs have been delayed and stretched. As a result, estimates of the investment bill alone, as recently as a year ago, suggested a total of $135 billion for the same five-year period.[10] The final budget for 1990 may bring this total down still further, largely because of proposed reductions in funding for the B-2 bomber and the strategic defense initiative.

Because strategic programs have long lead times, the large investments made during the 1980s have not yet greatly affected the triad of offensive forces. The number of ICBMs has fallen slightly; so has the size of the bomber force. Only the number of SLBM launchers has increased substantially. Because of this increase, however, what amounts to the substitution of the MX for the old Titan IIs, and the continued deployment of ALCMs on B-52 bombers, the number of warheads in the force has increased from approximately 9,000 to more than 12,500. As a result of these changes, and overestimates of the lethality of the Soviet SS-18 and SS-19 ICBMs, the second-strike performance of the offense should be, but probably is not, better than was estimated for the 1981 force (see table 9). However, the overall deterrent remains as sturdy as it was then. What is much less clear is whether any modest improvement in performance has been worth the greatly increased costs.

Future Directions

The issue of how much further we should go with many of the strategic programs is perhaps somewhat easier to resolve. Arguments about what the United States should target in the Soviet Union beyond cities are bound to continue. But given a history of nearly thirty years during which successive presidents have chosen to maintain options in addition to counter-city attacks, and given that retargeting does not seem to be a reliable mechanism while an attack is under way, the target list is likely to remain fairly long and the number of weapons dedicated to these targets fairly large, with control exercised by means of withholding certain weapons rather than retargeting a smaller number. This much granted, it is probable that the number of fixed hard targets will shrink somewhat during the next five years and that land-mobile Soviet missiles will prove difficult

10. Cindy Williams, "Strategic Spending Choices," in *International Security,* vol. 13 (Spring 1989), p. 30.

to attack. Consequently the number of targets that could be covered—regardless of how the exchange begins—is likely to grow smaller, while the number of targets that the president might choose not to attack (or not to attack in the first hours of an exchange) is likely to remain relatively constant (see table 8).

It also remains reasonably certain that neither the United States nor the Soviet Union will in the foreseeable future find a way to achieve and exploit a meaningful nuclear advantage or that either could escape from a nuclear exchange—even a limited one—without suffering millions of prompt fatalities. Both sides would therefore have strong incentives to avoid nuclear warfare but, should it somehow begin, to try to bring it to a halt as rapidly as possible and with minimum damage.

Countervailing. This concept, known in the past as a countervailing strategy, means, in effect, that the United States should be able to demonstrate that it could respond in kind (though not necessarily in numbers) to any kind of attack an enemy might undertake as well as to any follow-on strikes it might conduct. That in turn means that most forces should be survivable over a matter of days or even weeks so that there would be no incentive "to use them or lose them." And since any future arms reduction agreement is almost certain to be based on the principle of mutual deterrence, each side would presumably be expected (or allowed) to maintain a highly survivable reserve. After all is said and done, numerical parity is much less important than deterrence and stability.

Targeting. The general principles of a countervailing strategy provide one test of the utility of various strategic systems, with or without START. The specific makeup of the target list provides another. For example, if the Soviet Union were to plan, in a first strike, to attack U.S. missile silos, bomber bases, submarine ports, and air defenses, but withhold strikes against strategic communication centers, the appropriate U.S. response would be to fire at counterpart targets in the Soviet Union, even though many of those targets would be empty. If the Soviets were to follow this attempt at a disarming attack with strikes at other military and economic targets not heavily collocated with population in an effort to coerce a surrender, the United States should have the capability to retaliate in kind. Similarly, if at any point Soviet forces should start destroying cities, U.S. forces should be able to cause massive damage to a number of major Soviet cities. Under the vast majority of circumstances, one would expect an enemy to try first and foremost to disarm the United States; consequently the weapons needed to respond in kind do not have to be sustainably survivable. But since the opportunities for ending the destruction would probably be greatest after such an exchange, all other offensive forces should be capable of being withheld and of remaining survivable for a long time.

The triad and SLBMs. Finally, there is the issue of whether the maintenance of an offensive triad should determine the selection of strategic systems. There is, for example, a great deal of debate over the merits of particular ICBMs and penetrating bombers (versus cruise missile carriers); very little is said about the advantages of a triad over a dyad or about the price worth paying for a triad, even though SLBMs can perform all the functions of ICBMs and probably even those of penetrating bombers.

In light of these considerations, it is clear for the foreseeable future that SLBMs will constitute the backbone of the strategic offense. As many as 65 percent of them can be on station at any given moment, and they can remain undetected and survivable for extended periods. After a surprise attack or during a conflict, communications with them would be as good as with any other leg of the triad. And not only can they cover the full spectrum of fixed targets, hard or soft, but they can be easily withheld if the national command authorities so desire.

It is possible, given potential START constraints, that the Navy should consider building a submarine with 12 rather than 24 launchers, so as to be able to spread its share of the 4,900 ballistic missile warheads over a larger number of on-station boats. And the program for acquiring the D-5 (Trident II) is probably too ambitious considering that the number of hard targets is declining and that retaliation against those targets will be as much a demonstration that the attempt at a disarming attack has failed as an effort to destroy any remaining missiles or reloads. But a modern SLBM force, whatever its form, will be essential to deterrence for the remainder of the century.

Bombers. Despite the growing versatility of the SLBMs, prudence dictates some degree of diversity in the composition of the strategic offense, and bombers probably rank second to SLBMs in utility, reliability, and cost per second-strike-delivered warhead. They hold that rank not because they are recallable or because they can force an enemy to commit large resources to active defenses—yet still penetrate them. Nor is there much of a case that they can act as hunter-killers against land-mobile missiles or provide a unique threat to deep underground command centers, which the national command authorities may, in any event, wish to avoid. Their main virtues are, first, that they can be flown every day and thus are reliable in a sense that SLBMs and ICBMs never can be; and second, that armed with cruise missiles, they can penetrate enemy defenses without risking bombers or crews. However, because all the alert bombers would have to be launched on warning in order to survive, and would not be recallable except in a false alarm, they would have to be committed against the enemy's strategic forces (or whatever is left of the threat to Europe).

In the circumstances, despite its low alert rate—currently 30 percent in peacetime—it would seem sensible to keep the bomber fleet relatively small so as not to waste too many warheads on hard targets, to convert the B-1Bs to cruise missile carriers, and to hold the B-2 (Stealth) production to thirteen until the performance as well as the cost of the aircraft can be more fully evaluated. The same kind of decision may prove warranted for the advanced cruise missile (ACM), considering the rather undistinguished performance of Soviet air defenses against KAL 007, Matthias Rüst, and an unmanned MiG-23.[11]

ICBMs. The ICBM force has become the most controversial leg of the strategic triad, in part because of the expected vulnerability of silos, but also because it no longer is the only prompt hard-target killer and, like the SLBMs, would probably have to be fired from airborne command posts. Because of the first problem there are now two candidates to replace the Minuteman force: the rail-mobile MX and the land-mobile small ICBM (SICBM), also known as Midgetman. The rail-garrison MX would be the cheaper of the two systems, but it would allegedly be more vulnerable: it would be usually parked in known locations and would be a lucrative target because each missile would carry ten highly accurate warheads. Midgetman, on the other hand, would supposedly roam about on military reservations and carry only one (or perhaps two or three) warheads, which supposedly would make it less attractive as a target. However, there are indications that Midgetman would be extremely costly to operate and that the Air Force would choose to park it in garrisons as it plans to do with the MX and has done with the ground-launched cruise missile (now abolished by the INF Treaty).

A cheaper alternative would be to cancel the rail-garrison MX, continue development of the Midgetman missile but without any commitment to

---

11. In September 1983 a Soviet interceptor shot down KAL 007 over Sakhalin Island after a pursuit of thirty minutes. In May 1987 Matthias Rüst flew a single-engine Cessna aircraft undetected from West Germany to Red Square in Moscow. In the summer of 1989, after its Soviet pilot had bailed out over Poland, a MiG-23 flew unintercepted into West Germany, where U.S. fighters escorted it until it ran out of fuel and crashed.

produce it, and retain about 342 Minuteman III missiles in silos. These missiles, admittedly, would be vulnerable—given current estimates of Soviet SS-18 accuracy and reliability—but they would still present Soviet planners with the complication of trying to destroy the alert bombers and the ICBMs simultaneously. To complicate their task still further, the United States should insist in the START negotiations that the treaty ban all depressed trajectory firings of ballistic missiles from submarines.

Damage limiting. Defense planners will also have to decide, particularly with the resumption of the START negotiations, how far they want to proceed with a collection of programs that can be interpreted as an effort to nullify any Soviet strategic nuclear reserve while preserving one for the United States. They will also have to determine whether, in the current environment, they will get more of what they want in the way of mutual deterrence and stability by clinging to those programs (for bargaining or some other purpose) or by showing a willingness to moderate or even defer and cancel systems that could be obstacles to a satisfactory agreement.

The main suspects to an outside observer are easily identified. Granted its implausibility, a U.S. first strike with MX and D-5 (Trident II) missiles could cripple the Soviet silo-based ICBMs and bombers. At the same time B-2 aircraft could be on their way allegedly to seek out and destroy Soviet land-mobile missiles, while nuclear attack submarines, such as the improved SSN-688 and the new SSN-21, would be attempting to sink Soviet ballistic-missile submarines. And since not all these efforts would be successful, a deployed antiballistic missile (ABM) and antibomber defense could be deployed to intercept any relatively small or ragged retaliation. Or so a suspicious outside observer might infer from the current collection of U.S. offensive and defensive systems now in place or undergoing research and development.

The inference would probably be wrong on at least several counts. It would be hard to argue that the investment decisions of the past decade have been informed by a ''damage-limiting'' strategy, or by any strategic concept at all. Furthermore, by most accounts, not only would such a strategy fail, but it would also doom any prospect for mutual strategic deterrence and stability by means of a START agreement. Admittedly, all Soviet hard targets and bomber bases could be put in jeopardy. But it is highly doubtful that the B-2 would be of much use against land-mobile missiles or that the U.S. nuclear-attack submarines could be effective quickly enough to prevent a Soviet retaliation sufficient to saturate or exhaust any ABM defenses. In any event, agreement on a START treaty is likely to depend heavily on a willingness by the United States to curb the strategic defense initiative. Finally, there is the issue of money. When all direct and indirect costs are attributed to them, the strategic nuclear forces now entail outlays of about $52 billion a year, or more than 17 percent of total defense expenditures.[12] Even with the retirement of some older systems such as the B-52s, the Minuteman II ICBMs, and most Poseidon submarines, the addition of mobile ICBMs, the D-5 SLBM, the B-2, and an ABM deployment could easily raise those outlays to more than $87 billion by the end of the century. Exactly what would be accomplished by this increase in terms of deterrence and stability remains obscure.

A different approach would hold next-generation systems, such as the B-2, the rail-garrison MX, the small ICBM, and SDI, in research, development, test, and evaluation to find out what constitute their potentialities and operating and support costs (see tables 4 and 5). Meanwhile existing capabilities would be tailored more appropriately to the targets they are intended to cover and to the facilitation of a START treaty. The current overcommitment to weapons that could not be withheld and that would be targeted against Soviet strategic forces would be altered by converting the B1-B to a cruise missile carrier, phasing out the B-52s, mothballing the MX, and reducing the ICBM force to 342 Minuteman IIIs. The SSBN force would consist of 336 C-4 (Trident I) launchers and 192 D-5 (Trident II) launchers. The SDI would be funded at $3 billion a year, and all tests of its components would have to conform to the narrow interpretation of the ABM Treaty. A continental air defense system would also be retained, as would the current early warning, surveillance, and communications capabilities. Annual outlays for the force would come to $29.1 billion (see table 7).

The offensive component of the strategic forces under this reorientation would contain approximately 7,050 nuclear warheads, of which 4,224 would be in the submarine leg of the triad. The Soviets would still face the complication of having to attack both the ICBMs and the alert bombers. And despite the reductions in the force, the offense—after a well-executed Soviet surprise first strike—would still be able to deliver approximately 2,400 weapons on targets in the Soviet Union. Moreover, if the U.S. counteroffensive had been fully alerted as a result of a major crisis, the

12. See table 32 for a summary of U.S. forces and costs, 1990–99.

retaliation would consist of more than 3,800 delivered weapons. By 1994 this capability would cost $22.9 billion a year less that the current force. In other words, after a surprise attack the retaliatory capability of the force would decline by 30 percent, and the annual cost of the force would fall by more than 44 percent. Since fewer warheads would be wasted on hard targets, overall effectiveness would hardly change at all (see table 9).

Tactical Nuclear Forces

Not all U.S. nuclear weapons are concentrated in the strategic nuclear forces. About 10,000 of them are available for tactical use (see table 10). Few launchers are devoted exclusively to the delivery of these weapons. Most of the delivery systems consist of dual-capable artillery and aircraft, and ships and submarines that can carry a variety of nuclear as well as conventional warheads such as the controversial TLAM-N (Tomahawk land attack missile, nuclear). Most of the weapons are located in Europe, at sea, and in the continental United States. In addition, the United States has committed approximately 400 SLBM warheads against the nuclear threat to Europe.[13]

These delivery systems fall into three categories according to range: the battlefield capabilities that consist primarily of artillery; the short-range missiles that, for NATO, consist of Lance ballistic missiles with a range of about 110 kilometers; and the aircraft that can reach deep into Eastern Europe as well as the TLAM-N cruise missiles and C-3 ballistic missiles that can cover targets in the USSR as well as in Eastern Europe. Other intermediate-range land-based ballistic missiles are being destroyed in compliance with the INF Treaty.

The battlefield nuclear weapons were deployed to Western Europe nearly forty years ago on two assumptions: that enemy forces would have to concentrate to break through NATO's defenses, and that a first use of nuclear weapons by NATO would destroy these concentrations and thereby act as a substitute for the conventional forces that NATO lacked. These assumptions might have fallen into disrepute as the Soviet Union began to accumulate a stockpile of nuclear weapons and short-range delivery systems of its own. Instead, NATO expanded its idea of a tactical nuclear

---

13. For the origins of this commitment, see William W. Kaufmann, *The McNamara Strategy* (Harper and Row, 1964), p. 107.

war to include the use of nuclear weapons not only against troops but also against airfields, missile sites, and lines of communications. In effect, NATO planners came to visualize a traditional military campaign in which nuclear weapons would substitute for conventional firepower in rear areas as well as on the battlefield. As this expansion occurred, so did the demand for nuclear warheads and various types of delivery systems. Roughly 7,000 nuclear bombs and shells were deployed in response, as were dual-capable aircraft, Honest John, Lance, and Pershing I missiles.[14]

The concurrent growth in the Soviet nuclear arsenal, the deployment by the Soviets of medium- and intermediate-range missiles and bombers, the flight of Sputnik, and the crisis over the credibility of the U.S. nuclear deterrent led eventually to further changes in NATO's nuclear concepts and forces. Despite Soviet capabilities, NATO clung to the belief that it could and would be the first to use nuclear weapons. The United States also put forward the idea of a multilateral nuclear force and pledged to use 400 SLBM warheads against the missiles and bombers in the USSR that constituted a threat to Western Europe. And in an effort to link the U.S. strategic deterrent to the defense of Western Europe and to demonstrate that an attack on NATO, if continued, would inevitably lead to the use of that deterrent, planners visualized a process of escalation requiring U.S. delivery systems based in Western Europe that could reach well into the Soviet Union itself. Hence the deployment of the Army's Pershing II ballistic missile and the Air Force's ground-launched cruise missile, followed by much dismay in some quarters at the ratification of the INF Treaty, which requires the destruction of those missiles, and by efforts to find a substitute for them.

Several points about this evolution are worth noting. In recent years NATO defense analysts have asserted (with considerable justification) that Soviet nuclear capabilities in Europe have substantially exceeded those of the Western allies; yet these same allies have insisted that they would have the will to use nuclear weapons first and, if necessary, to escalate the range and weight of these attacks. Of late, in fact, more emphasis has gone to the threat of escalating than to the conduct of a nuclear campaign, and SACEUR (supreme allied commander, Europe) has indicated that he values a follow-on to the aging Lance missile more highly than his battlefield nuclear capabilities. In the meantime very little thought has been

---

14. For a review of these policies, see John J. Midgley, Jr., *Deadly Illusions: Army Policy for the Nuclear Battlefield* (Westview Press, 1986).

given to the possibility that the Soviet Union might preempt a NATO first use or to the vulnerability of NATO's nuclear capabilities to conventional as well as to nuclear attack.

Possible changes in or modernization of these capabilities are unlikely to have a major impact on U.S. defense spending one way or another. But they do raise several issues that will affect both the START and CFE negotiations. The Federal Republic of Germany would like to strike an agreement with the Soviet Union that would get rid of all short-range missiles in Europe, and Gorbachev seems eager to consummate such a deal even though the USSR would give up far more missiles and warheads than NATO. The Bush administration and other governments fear that such a step would lead to the eventual denuclearization of Europe and severance of the link between the U.S. strategic nuclear forces and the defense of Western Europe. Therefore, they have proposed to defer any negotiations on short-range missiles until the talks on conventional force reductions and stability have been completed on what is hoped will be an accelerated schedule. Even then, however, they oppose a complete ban on short-range missiles comparable to the INF Treaty. Proceeding to this third "zero," they believe would be going too far, since even in a stable conventional environment, and even if battlefield nuclear weapons were left in place, the deterrent to a conventional attack would be reduced. Conventional stability, they argue, has not prevented past conventional wars.

However that argument may be resolved, the issue remains of whether or how the Lance missile, now thirty years old, should be modernized. Several options are available. One is simply to upgrade the existing missile. The difficulty with this choice is that, because of the short range of the Lance, its warheads would land on German soil and punish Germans more than Russians. Other options would, while adhering to the 300-mile limit imposed by the INF Treaty, be able to hit targets in Poland. The two most popular choices for this mission are TASM (tactical air-to-surface missile), which could be a modified SRAM II (short-range attack missile) already under development for U.S. strategic bombers, and FOTL (follow-on-to Lance), which would consist of a nuclear missile launched from the Army's MLRS (multiple-launch rocket system), a conventional system already being deployed to U.S. and allied forces in Europe. One problem with FOTL is that any future negotiation to remove short-range nuclear missiles from Europe might compromise the conventional deployment of the MLRS—one of the Army's better new weapons—because of difficulties in distinguishing between a conventional and a nuclear MLRS and hence an agreement to ban the entire system.

Still another option, one that has become entangled in the START negotiations, is the sea-launched nuclear cruise missile known as TLAM-N. The Navy plans to acquire 758 of the nuclear version of the Tomahawk, as well as more than 3,000 of the conventional version.[15] Furthermore, the Navy is already deploying both versions on surface combatants as well as on submarines. As of now, the TLAM is a troublesome system: the nuclear and conventional versions of it are indistinguishable except by highly intrusive measures of inspection, its range is more than 1,000 miles, and because it is based at sea, it is not covered by the INF Treaty. The Soviet Union would like to include TLAM in the START negotiations and abolish both versions. The Navy is determined to keep both versions but is unwilling to commit the TLAM-N either to the SIOP (the single integrated operational plan) for the strategic nuclear forces or to SA-CEUR's general strike plan for the nuclear forces under his command in Europe. As a consequence, and because of the primary missions of the ships and submarines on which TLAM-N is based, these missiles cannot be counted on for a coordinated or timely response in the event of a nuclear emergency. The Navy seems to see them as a kind of general nuclear reserve force.

A different basing mode for the TLAM-N might solve both the problem of covering targets in Eastern Europe and the issue of verification. The United States is now retiring some of its Poseidon submarines as more Trident boats enter the strategic force. Without any violation of existing treaties or understandings, as many as ten of the older submarines could be modified to carry cruise missiles (as the Soviet Oscar class does), and all TLAM-Ns could be transferred to these platforms. Such a transfer would accomplish two purposes. First, it would permit a clear and logical distinction between the nuclear and the conventional versions of the TLAM. Second, it would give SACEUR a dedicated force of on-station missiles that would cover targets of importance to his command and at the same time remove the dangers of any political explosion that might accompany a decision to provide a land-based follow-on to Lance. The cost of such a modification, moreover, would be modest—probably no more that $300 million per submarine. And even with such a change, the total annual

15. Richard K. Betts, *Cruise Missiles and U.S. Policy* (Brookings, 1982), pp. 7–8.

cost of the tactical nuclear forces—warheads as well as dedicated delivery systems—would not run to more than $3.5 billion (see table 11).

Conventional Forces

The conventional forces of the United States represent a much higher order of cost. When investment, operations, and direct and indirect support are charged to these forces, they comprise 80 percent or more of defense outlays. For nearly thirty years the Pentagon has justified such a large effort on two grounds: first, that it would raise the nuclear threshold, and second, that it was the price of having to support allies in Europe and Asia against simultaneous attacks launched by the Soviet Union and its allies with little or no warning. Thus arose what became known in the 1960s as the 2½ and thereafter (with the change in Chinese policy) as the 1½ war strategy.

These descriptions have oversimplified both the apparent objectives of the Joint Chiefs of Staff and the demands that would be made on U.S. conventional forces in a major emergency. Should a war-threatening crisis arise in Europe, for example, U.S. ground and tactical air forces would attempt to deploy, or reinforce deployed forces (as in Germany and Korea), in seven different theaters with a total of thirty-two division forces and forty-one fighter-attack wings drawn from the active and reserve Army, Marine Corps, and Air Force. Efforts to mobilize large quantities of airlift and sealift would be made to ensure the timely deployment of the fighting units. In addition, the Navy would be called upon to help control the major sea lines of communications to Europe, the Mediterranean, Northeast Asia, and the Persian Gulf and would probably seek to launch several power projection operations with its carrier battle groups and Marine amphibious forces in areas such as North Norway and Thrace.[16]

Whatever one may think of this strategy—which, at least initially, would constitute a holding action—current U.S. capabilities, practically speaking, are not sufficient to meet these multiple and more or less simultaneous demands. The strategy depends on high readiness and rapid response not only in the active-duty but also in the large reserve forces now maintained by the United States. Yet, though current ground and

16. See table 12 for national defense outlays by force planning contingencies.

tactical air forces are nearly adequate in force size and composition for their missions, their reserve components (in the National Guard and Reserve), on which they have come to depend so heavily, could probably not meet the standards of readiness and deployability that the strategy seems to require. Equally troublesome, especially given the very conservative assumption that the USSR would attack in several theaters at once and that cohorts such as North Korea and Cuba would join in the fray— all after only a few days of usable warning—airlift and sealift would be in short supply, despite the efforts of the Air Force to obtain 66 million ton-miles of airlift a day, an increase in the Navy's sealift, and the prepositioning of heavy equipment and supplies both on land and at sea in Europe, the Indian Ocean, and Northeast Asia.[17] To make matters worse, the Navy—because of its emphasis on carrier battle groups, power projection, and amphibious operations—would probably have more carrier battle groups on hand than it would know what to do with and too few escorts and mine warfare ships for the less glamorous but more critical tasks of protecting convoys of reinforcement and supplies needed to sustain forces in widely dispersed theaters. But even supposing that all these proposed deployments could take place, that forward defenses could be established in the key theaters, and that the principal sea-lanes could be adequately protected, there would probably be a shortage of the war reserve stocks needed to sustain overseas operations long enough to permit adequate support from existing or expanded production lines in the United States, especially if simultaneous conflicts were in progress.

There are, in principle, several ways to reduce this mismatch between supply and demand without any major change in the strategy. One obvious recourse would be to insist that U.S. allies in Europe and Asia contribute much more than they now do to the collective defense. Unfortunately, even in much grimmer times, this kind of arm-twisting has not enjoyed a great deal of success, especially since American commanders have continued to proclaim the merits of nuclear weapons. In the kinder and gentler days of Gorbachev such appeals and demands are even less likely to obtain a positive response. Indeed, the response might well go in a more negative direction.

Another way to fill the gap would be to expand certain capabilities such as airlift and sealift, increase land- and sea-based pre-positioning,

17. *Budget of the United States Government, Fiscal Year 1990*, p. 5-10.

and substitute still more quality for quantity by rapid strides in weapons technology and a speedier turnover of weapons and equipment in the conventional inventory. This is the option that the services probably favor, with the early introduction by the Army of new helicopters, new forward area air defenses, new tank armor and antiarmor weapons; by the Navy of a new destroyer, more advanced aircraft carriers, an advanced tactical aircraft, a tilt-rotor transport aircraft for the Marines, and a newer and bigger nuclear attack submarine; and by the Air Force of an advanced tactical fighter, a much modified version of the F-15 fighter, new versions of the F-16 fighter, and an airlift aircraft (the C-17A) intended to operate efficiently as both an intercontinental and an intratheater transporter—just as the C-5A was intended to do many years ago. Regrettably, however, the gap between military supply and demand is likely to be matched by the gap between programs and resources. Indeed, despite the efforts of the last two years, it would appear that current programs are underfunded by at least $80 billion during the 1990–94 five-year defense program.[18] Accordingly, even if quality could be substituted as readily for quantity as these programs suggest (a doubtful proposition), this option would not be in the cards.

A third way to deal with the problem would take Soviet arms reductions with the utmost seriousness and have the Pentagon make reciprocal moves of its own. If such an approach appears to surrender too many bargaining chips or to jeopardize U.S. security, it is worth recalling what Gorbachev is already doing without any bargaining at all. He is reducing Soviet ground and tactical air forces by 500,000 men, taking out from East Germany, Czechoslovakia, and Hungary 50,000 of this total and 6 tank divisions. He is also pushing the Soviet military to adopt a doctrine of "nonoffensive defense" to replace the current strategy of preemptive conventional attack into Western Europe or, failing that, "a counter offensive with overwhelming artillery and mechanized forces."[19] Perhaps of greater interest, he and his prime minister, Nikolai I. Ryzhkov, have begun to talk more specifically about the Soviet defense budget and how they propose to cut it. Although the figures used by the two men do not quite agree, Gorbachev maintains that defense spending has not increased since 1987 and that he plans to reduce it by 14.2 percent by 1991. Ryzhkov goes even further

18. See tables 4 and 5 for reductions in major procurement and RDT&E, 1990–94.
19. Bernard E. Trainor, *New York Times,* March 7, 1988, pp. A1, A9.

and talks of cutting defense spending by a third to a half over the next six years.[20] All these steps are worth encouraging, not by increasing U.S. defense spending and the modernization of its forces, but by relaxing to some degree the U.S. effort. To go further, the opportunity now exists to reconcile U.S. strategy with U.S. forces and budgets.

At this point there is no need, with certain exceptions, to drop any of the contingencies for which the Pentagon has been planning. Instead, in this period of transition, it seems reasonable to assume much less simultaneity in their occurrence—perhaps only one at a time—and much more time in which to prepare for any large attack. At present, for example, defense planners assume that, at best, they will have ten days of usable warning before a major Pact assault on Western Europe. That, in turn, means a heavy dependence on pre-positioned equipment, airlift, and metronomic precision in force deployments, and it demands high readiness in both active and reserve forces. However, as the Soviets withdraw crack divisions from Eastern Europe, while East Germany, Czechoslovakia, Bulgaria, Poland, and Hungary announce reductions in their conventional forces, the probability of a large, short-warning attack declines appreciably.[21] Instead of ten days, something on the order of ninety days of usable warning seems plausible. That means more of an opportunity to bring reserve forces up to active standards of readiness, to discontinue efforts to expand pre-positioning and airlift, and to place greater reliance on sealift. Indeed, in light of the weapons-counting rules under consideration at the CFE negotiations in Vienna, where the Soviets insist that U.S. pre-positioned equipment be included in the totals, it might make sense to return some of that equipment to the United States and give it to the National Guard and Reserve rather than fund additional weapons for those forces.

Although it would probably be a mistake to reduce ground and tactical air forces below current levels, it would be difficult to make the same case for the Navy. Admittedly, Marshal Sergei F. Akhromeyev, Gorbachev's closest military adviser, has indicated a Soviet determination to negotiate a reduction in naval forces, and especially in U.S. large-deck aircraft carriers, which may cause resistance to any unilateral change in

20. See table 13 for published Soviet defense outlays in 1989. See also *Washington Post*, June 8, 1989, pp. A25, A27, for planned reductions in Soviet defense spending.

21. For East European plans, see U.S. Arms Control and Disarmament Agency, *Arms Control Update*, no. 12 (March 3, 1989), p. 6; and *Arms Control Reporter, 1989* (Institute for Defense and Disarmament Studies), pp. 407.B, 115–28.

the size and composition of the U.S. Navy.[22] But it is also true that the Navy has failed to justify in any persuasive way the acquisition of fifteen deployable carrier battle groups or of the amphibious lift for an additional Marine brigade. Indeed, Secretary of Defense Cheney has already reduced the number of deployable carriers by one (to fourteen), and twelve deployable carrier battle groups and a division's worth of amphibious lift seem more than enough for any power projection missions the Navy might be called on to perform in the near future. Furthermore, such a reduction would still leave ample room for further negotiations with the Russians, should naval forces be put on the bargaining table.

There are also several grounds for questioning the need to introduce a new generation of costly conventional weapons at this time. Ordinarily, defense rolls over its inventory of weapons, on the average, every twenty years and spends a great deal of money upgrading the existing inventory in between. Now, however, the services—without yet having completed the acquisition of the generation of weapons introduced in the mid-1970s— is attempting to field follow-on capabilities that will be even more expensive in real terms to buy, operate, and maintain. Besides, these new weapons, many of which are undergoing concurrent test, evaluation, and production, are designed to deal with threats that may well vanish under the pressure of massive Soviet deficits, defense budget cuts, and the reductions in arms that Gorbachev so badly needs. In the circumstances it seems plausible to follow the old policy of "fly before buy" with such systems as the Army's light helicopter family and forward area air defenses, the Navy's new nuclear attack submarine and guided missile destroyer, the Marines' tilt-rotor aircraft (which Secretary Cheney has tried to cancel), and three very sophisticated aircraft: the Navy's advanced tactical aircraft, and the Air Force's advanced tactical fighter and its C-17A airlift aircraft (see tables 4 and 5). Few of these systems deserve outright cancellation without further test and evaluation. None should be considered for production (or further production) until 1995. By then, we should see more clearly how far the Soviets are prepared to go in ending the arms competition and to what extent, if any, U.S. conventional forces will need the next generation of, by then, well-tested weapons.

The net result of modest reductions in personnel and operating costs (because of conventional force cuts and slightly lower readiness) and important changes in investment strategy would be a decline in outlays

22. *New York Times*, July 25, 1989, p. A9.

of $13.6 billion by 1994, or a reduction of approximately 12 percent in outlays for the conventional forces (see table 15). Resources for defense-wide intelligence and communications and for retired pay accrual would not be affected by these changes. Military pay and operation and main-tenance, on the other hand, would decline because of the force reductions. But pay would keep pace with inflation over the five-year period.[23]

Overall, as a result of the changes proposed in both nuclear and con-ventional capabilities, defense outlays would fall, in real terms, from just under $300 billion in 1990 to $265 billion in 1994. The cut of $35 billion would represent a real decline of just over 13 percent for the entire period and an annual cut of a little more than 3 percent, which contrasts with Secretary Cheney's request for increases averaging slightly more than 1.7 percent a year in real terms.[24] Barring a startling change in the international environment, it is difficult to see how the proposed reductions would decrease the conditions of U.S. security. It is even conceivable that co-operation with the Soviet Union to this extent (with or without Gorbachev) would actually increase stability and with it the security of the nation.

23. See tables 14 and 19 for changes in personnel and reductions in military pay and operation and maintenance.

24. See tables 3 and 19 for the Cheney outlays and those of the reduced FYDP.

CHAPTER THREE

START AND CFE AGREEMENTS AND THEIR IMPLICATIONS, 1995–97

A NATIONAL defense program leading to outlays of $265 billion by 1994 should give a strong signal of the U.S. desire to proceed with stable reductions in forces and budgets and assist Gorbachev in his manifest desire to switch resources from the military to the civilian sector of the Soviet economy, yet hedge against a breakdown of the process. Whether it will become possible to sustain deterrence and military stability at still lower levels of defense spending will depend on what comes out of the negotiations on START and CFE.

START Constraints

Although a number of disagreements over the strategic nuclear forces need to be ironed out, what constraints a START agreement will place on these forces are reasonably clear. The United States and the Soviet Union will each be limited to a maximum of 1,600 strategic nuclear delivery vehicles (bombers, ICBMs, and SLBMs). These vehicles will carry no more that 6,000 ''accountable'' nuclear warheads, of which a maximum of 4,900 will be allocated to long-range ballistic missiles. In addition, the USSR will reduce its very heavy SS-18 ICBMs from 308 to 154, with 1,540 warheads. And total ballistic missile throw-weight on each side will be set at 50 percent of the Soviet level as of either December 31, 1986 (the U.S. proposal), or the date on which a START treaty is signed (the Soviet proposal). This constraint will presumably affect only the USSR, since Soviet ballistic missile throw-weight is at least double that of the United States.[25]

25. See table 20 for the status of the strategic arms reduction talks as of June 1989.

Bombers would be treated differently from ballistic missiles. A bomber equipped with gravity bombs and short-range attack missiles would count as only one strategic nuclear delivery vehicle and one warhead, presumably because it would not constitute much of a threat as a first-strike weapon (though that might not be true of the B-2 if it is able to penetrate Soviet defenses without being detected). On the other hand, a bomber loaded with air-launched cruise missiles would count as one strategic nuclear delivery vehicle, but its armament would count either as ten warheads no matter how many cruise missiles were being carried (the U.S. position), or as the maximum number of cruise missiles the bomber could carry (the Soviet position).

No doubt the negotiations will result in still further rules and regulations. Conceivably, a ban on depressed trajectory firings will be introduced. Marshal Akhromeyev has also proposed a limit on the total number of air-launched cruise missiles to be deployed and seems to have indicated a willingness to trade the Soviet rail-mobile heavy missile with ten warheads (the SS-24) for the U.S. rail-garrison MX with ten warheads. There also remain the issues of the limits to be imposed on the strategic defense initiative and sea-launched cruise missiles.[26]

Implications of START

Interestingly enough, the reduced five-year defense program proposed for 1990–94 sets the stage for one possible resolution of these last two issues. Furthermore, the strategic nuclear forces contained in the program come fairly close to fitting within the main constraints of START. The number of strategic nuclear delivery vehicles is 960, well below the proposed treaty limit of 1,600. However, the number of "accountable" warheads is (on the Soviet interpretation) 7,050—instead of 6,000—and there are too many ballistic missile warheads—5,250 instead of 4,900.[27] More bombers could be added to bring the number of strategic nuclear delivery vehicles to 1,600, but the increase would not be worth the cost, especially since warheads would have to be taken away from other and more pro-

26. The Soviet Union has now indicated that it would sign a START treaty without an agreement on ABM limits, but would be free to abrogate the treaty if the United States deviated from the strict interpretation of the ABM accord.

27. See tables 7 and 9 for U.S. strategic nuclear launchers and warheads, fiscal 1990–99.

ductive systems. Whether, in fact, the force can be adjusted to the warhead constraints is by far the more challenging issue.

To make the adjustment would suggest changing slightly the allocation between ICBMs and SLBMs and keeping the remainder of the force approximately as previously proposed (see tables 7 and 9). Thus the B-1B and tanker force would remain constant, the Minuteman III ICBMs would be reduced by 53 (or 159 warheads), 8 Poseidon boats with 1,024 warheads would be retired, and the Trident submarines would be increased to 19 (from 16), with 3,648 warheads. The total number of warheads in the redesigned force would fall from 7,050 to 6,443; the "accountable" number of warheads would stand at 5,723; and ballistic missile warheads would come to 4,643, with 3,648 aboard Trident SLBMs. Such a force would cost $27.7 billion a year, $1.4 billion less than its hypothetical predecessor (see tables 7 and 9).

Depending on the outcome of both the START and CFE negotiations, the second-strike target list for the U.S. strategic nuclear forces could shrink to 2,800 or fewer separate aiming points (see table 8). The revised, START-constrained U.S. offense should be able, even after a surprise Soviet first strike, to deliver 2,184 warheads against these aiming points with a damage expectancy of better than 75 percent (see table 9). Although the triad would be preserved, the ICBMs, because of their vulnerability, would provide only 2 percent of the delivered warheads, whereas the ALCMs would furnish 18 percent and the SLBMs 81 percent. As a consequence, there would be ample prompt hard-target-kill capability, yet more than 58 percent of the warheads could be withheld if the president so decided. Depending on the choices made by the Soviets, stability would be maintained, deterrence strengthened, and costs slightly lowered.

Constraints on Conventional Forces in Europe

Compared with START, the CFE talks, or what are now formally entitled Negotiations on Conventional Armed Forces in Europe (NO-CAFE), raise a nightmare of complications. Europe, for the purposes of the negotiations, is defined as extending from the Atlantic to the Urals (ATTU), and the participants in the talks consist of the members of NATO and the Warsaw Pact (or Warsaw Treaty Organization). The mandate of the negotiations does not include U.S. and Canadian forces in other parts of the world or Soviet conventional capabilities east of the Ural mountains.

For the time being all naval forces are excluded from the agenda, although the Soviets include some of them in their weapons inventories for both NATO and the Warsaw Pact.

The units of account that were supposed to be the subject of negotiation were ground force weapons—and particularly main battle tanks, artillery, and armored troop carriers. But the Soviets have insisted on including personnel, aircraft, and helicopters as well. Each alliance has therefore provided a list of what it believes the two sides deploy in these categories within the ATTU region. Unfortunately the two inventories do not fully agree, in part because of differing definitions of what constitute tanks or artillery, for example, and in part because the parties disagree on what should be counted. NATO excludes its "covered" or pre-positioned equipment from its inventory; the Warsaw Pact provides a listing of interceptor aircraft, but argues that they are defensive weapons and should not be a subject of the negotiations.

These inventories are important for several reasons. They provide the baseline from which agreed reductions are to be made, and they indicate the number of weapons that will have to be destroyed and the number of people that will have to be demobilized to reach negotiated limits. Both sides also agree that the two inventories should become equal and then be equally reduced some 10 percent or 15 percent below the original level of parity. Thus, according to the Soviet inventory, NATO has 30,690 tanks, and the Warsaw Pact has 59,470. To achieve equality in the ATTU area, the Pact would have to destroy 28,780 of its tanks; a 15 percent reduction below the NATO total would require each side to destroy 4,604 tanks, although Gorbachev has actually offered to cut the Pact total by 40,000. That would mean a nearly 37 percent reduction from the NATO total, or 19,470 tanks on each side in the ATTU area, which is close to what NATO is proposing as the limit on main battle tanks in the same area, though from a smaller inventory for NATO (22,224) as well as the Pact (57,300).[28]

Both sides, in addition to specifying limits for the entire ATTU area, have divided it into three zones and specified limits on the number of weapons in the various categories that can be located in each zone. But the zones defined by the two sides do not coincide. The purpose of having such zones is nonetheless clear: to ensure that, of the total number of weapons allowed in the ATTU area, no more than a certain proportion

28. See table 21 for Warsaw Pact data on armed forces in Europe, January 30, 1989.

can be concentrated in a particular zone. As one example, NATO has proposed that each alliance be allowed 20,000 main battle tanks, 16,500 artillery pieces, and 28,000 armored troop carriers in the ATTU area. However, in the same proposal, no more than 8,000 tanks, 4,500 artillery pieces, and 11,000 armored troop carriers would be allowed in active units in the sensitive zone consisting of the Netherlands, Belgium, Luxembourg, West Germany, East Germany, Czechoslovakia, and Poland. The danger of a sudden concentration of forces would thus be reduced. To strengthen these constraints, no one country in either alliance would be allowed more than 12,000 main battle tanks, 10,000 artillery pieces, and 16,800 armored troop carriers in the ATTU area, and no member of either alliance would station more than 3,200 main battle tanks, 1,700 artillery pieces, and 6,000 armored troop carriers in active units outside its own territory.[29]

Despite many differences over units of account, the baseline numbers from which reductions are to be made, and the zones into which the ATTU area is to be divided, both sides hope to reach an agreement within a year. Whether it will establish "a secure and stable balance of conventional forces at lower levels" and eliminate "the capability for launching surprise and for initiating large-scale offensive action" is even less certain.[30] Part of the reason for this uncertainty is that the units of account being used make it difficult to obtain a clear picture of what the proposed reductions would signify militarily. Nor do these numbers help to determine whether reductions would result in any change in U.S. defense outlays (since substitution possibilities would be large). It may help, therefore, to return to such traditional and visible units of account as division forces and fighter-attack wings, since they encompass both weapons and people. It also makes sense to focus on the central region of Europe (since that is where most of the U.S. ground and tactical air forces are or would be concentrated). It would pay to assess the current military situation there and how, in traditional terms, stability at reduced levels could be achieved— and achieved in such a way that it would take more than a year to upset the stalemate.

Although there are many disputes about the stability of the existing military situation in central Europe, and the analyses on which these opinions are based remain a source of still further disagreements, the

29. See table 22 for NATO-proposed conventional limits from the Atlantic to the Urals.
30. *Arms Control Update*, no. 12, p. 4.

majority view for some time has been that the Warsaw Pact would have a large military advantage whether in a surprise attack or after a major mobilization and deployment of its forces—a process that might take three or four months. Indeed, this view seems to be borne out by the Soviet willingness to make much larger reductions in its weapons inventories than NATO. No wonder that most SACEURs, however unrealistically, have claimed that they would have to use nuclear weapons against Pact forces within a matter of days after the beginning of an attack.

Despite what has been characterized as a Warsaw Pact advantage of better than 2:1—an advantage calculated long before Gorbachev's announcement of unilateral troop reductions by the Soviet Union—how well the Warsaw Pact forces would perform remains uncertain.[31] It is not at all clear, for example, that the Soviet Union would want to or could logistically support offensive operations against Norway, Greece, and Turkey as well as against the central region (that is, West Germany), especially since, if the central region were to collapse, the rest of Europe would almost certainly come under Soviet control without much of a fight. In addition, there has always been a question about the reliability of the East European forces, which would contribute up to a third of the Pact's attack capability, and that question must loom even larger now as Poland, Hungary, East Germany, and Czechoslovakia move toward greater self-determination. Finally, it is hard to determine whether NATO superiority in offensive airpower would be sufficient to counterbalance the Pact's numerical advantage on the ground. What is reasonably clear, however, is that the Soviets are deeply concerned about NATO's fighter-attack aircraft and that they will insist on including them, as well as military personnel, in any agreement on conventional force reductions. In sum, the Vienna talks will probably end up negotiating as much about active and reserve divisions and air wings as about such categories of weapons as main battle tanks, artillery pieces, and armored troop carriers.

As a matter of fact, President Bush has already recognized this trend. He has wisely agreed to include both aircraft and personnel in the Vienna negotiations. In his speech to NATO on May 29, 1989, he offered to reduce the U.S. military presence in Western Europe from 305,000 to 275,000 provided the Soviet Union would also reduce its forces in Eastern Europe to 275,000. Overall, the U.S. reduction would amount to more than 8 percent, but the president proposed that the 30,000 men be taken

---

31. See table 24 for the official view of the conventional balance in central Europe in 1987.

from ground and air combat forces (rather than from combat service support personnel) and that the personnel be demobilized and their equipment destroyed. He also proposed concluding an agreement in six to twelve months and effecting the necessary cuts by 1992 or 1993.[32]

Because the president's initiatives have broadened the scope of the Vienna negotiations, several questions arise in trying to define conventional military stability at lower levels than now exist in the central region of Europe. First, how many divisions (which are more easily countable than weapons) would the Warsaw Pact have to get rid of—along with their equipment—to lower the probability of a successful attack to 50 percent or less against existing NATO active and reserve capabilities? Second, granted the uncertainties about the effectiveness of modern fighter-attack aircraft, how many (if any) would NATO have to give up to ensure (if they were used optimally to suppress Pact offensive and defensive airpower and attack Soviet reinforcements) that NATO would not obtain better than a 50 percent probability of both halting a Pact attack and taking the offensive? Third, since both sides agree that all forces should be reduced below current NATO levels, what are the lowest levels that would be acceptable to NATO defense planners and what would be the basis for that judgment?

In the central region, including France and Denmark, and counting reserve as well as active units, NATO currently has in place a maximum capability of approximately 45.4 divisions (or the equivalent of 30⅓ U.S. armored divisions, using U.S. Army assessments of the combat power of these divisions) and approximately 1,707 fighter-attack aircraft. The Warsaw Pact, by comparison, could deploy 110 divisions (or 84 U.S. armored division equivalents) and 1,780 fighter-attack aircraft. In other words, after a significant period of mobilization and deployment—but without any reinforcements from the United States, which could amount to as many as 17 more large divisions—the Warsaw Pact would have almost a 2.8:1 advantage on the ground, and a 1.04:1 advantage in fighter-attack aircraft.[33]

Based on an effort to quantify military judgments about the results of such force relationships (one of many ways to model the interaction of conventional capabilities, and using combat power, effectiveness, and

---

32. *New York Times*, May 29, 1989, pp. A1, A6, and May 30, 1989, p. A13.

33. See table 25 for NATO and Warsaw Pact ground and fighter-attack forces in 1990 and after two stages of CFE reductions.

ratios of combat power as the main determinants of performance), the answer to the first question seems to be that the Warsaw Pact would have to dismantle approximately 70.7 divisions to achieve stability, of which 34 would come out of East Germany, Czechoslovakia, and Poland, 23 out of the three western military districts of the Soviet Union (the Baltic, Byelorussian, and Carpathian), and 13⅔ out of the strategic reserve of 20 divisions in the Moscow and Volga military districts (or a total of 54 U.S. armored division equivalents).

As for the second question, to allay Soviet concerns and ensure stability on the ground, assuming that NATO aircraft could quickly gain air superiority and successfully attack Warsaw Pact follow-on forces, the West might agree to leave the Pact interceptor force at its current level of numbers and modernization and, in return, require both sides—as a first step—to reduce their fighter-attack forces to 1,500 aircraft. Such a reduction in aircraft and ground forces would leave NATO capabilities in the central region with 45.4 divisions (of which no more than 30 would be active duty), or 30⅓ armored division equivalents and nearly 21 fighter-attack wings. By comparable measures, the Pact would field 39⅓ divisions (or 30⅓ armored division equivalents), and the U.S. equivalent of about 21 fighter-attack wings. These orders of battle would include 6 U.S. division equivalents and 29⅓ Soviet divisions, of which 13 would remain stationed in East Germany, Czechoslovakia, and Poland—surely enough to keep the area under control (see table 25).

By how much further these forces could be reduced while maintaining military stability depends on several factors: the length of the front being defended; the appropriate ratio of ground forces to space (that is, the number of troops per linear kilometer); the time required to move forces into their emergency war positions; and the willingness to give up a solidly manned front in favor of a war of maneuver, with the possibility of exposed flanks on both sides.

The NATO front in the central region of Europe effectively constitutes the border of West Germany, which runs to about 900 kilometers. Where to place the actual zone of defense is a function of many factors, including political decisions about how far forward to make a stand. For purposes of illustration, it is assumed here that the defense line would cover 750 kilometers, parts of which would lie in difficult terrain and could be held with relatively few forces. At issue is how densely the front should be manned to prevent a penetration without the attacker having to concentrate a superior force against a particular sector of the front, and thus not only warning the defender of an impending attack but also enabling it to rein-force the threatened sector. Under modern conditions a U.S. division on the defense might occupy a front ranging anywhere from 18 kilometers (a solid position) to 45 kilometers (a porous position), depending on the kind of terrain and any natural or man-made obstacles.

At present neither NATO nor the Warsaw Pact occupies more than a part of its emergency war positions. Thus a movement to man the front and deploy reserves should be readily detected. Following a general alert, NATO would probably try to cover the front with some 30 divisions, which on average would give each division a responsibility for 25 kilo-meters of frontage. If the Warsaw Pact deployed in roughly the same fashion, neither side would have much of a reserve once the CFE cuts had been made. However, a gambling attacker with the initiative might try to thin out portions of its front and try in secrecy to concentrate enough forces to effect a breakthrough and classical encircling movements. The defender could of course reply by thinning out its own front in order to reinforce the threatened sector, but such action would take time and could result in a misallocation of resources, especially if the attacker had feinted in other areas before revealing its main point of attack. In this sense, even roughly equivalent forces at the current NATO level combined with rea-sonably dense force-to-space ratios would not necessarily prevent a war of maneuver or ensure military stability in a crisis.

What all this suggests, particularly in light of the intent to reduce forces on both sides at least 10–15 percent below the current NATO level, and President Bush's pledge to remove 30,000 U.S. combat troops (under certain conditions), is that while they are important, force-to-space ratios do not provide a conclusive answer to where the floor should be set on ground and tactical air reductions. Instead, it would seem feasible to make reductions beyond those already outlined provided that substitutes for solid fronts were put in place. Such substitutes would include frequent ex-changes of information and random inspections, the use of air and ground sensors, controls on exercises and maneuvers, and the design of prepared defenses.

Assuming such measures were instituted, what would be the implica-tions of a reduction of 15 percent below current NATO levels in the central region? NATO ground forces would fall from 45.4 to 39 divisions (or 25⅔ U.S. armored division equivalents), and from 1,500 to 1,275 fighter-attack aircraft (or over 17⅔ wings). Warsaw Pact ground forces would go down from 39⅓ to 33⅓ divisions (also equal to 25⅔ U.S. armored division equivalents), and from 1,500 to 1,275 fighter-attack aircraft (or slightly more than the equivalent of 17⅔ U.S. wings). In these circumstances not only would a large concentration of forces (including both active and reserve units) take a lot of time, but any attack would run high risks in the face of inspection and other measures.

Besides such reductions, the United States has proposed that American forces stationed in Western Europe and Soviet forces garrisoned in East Germany, Czechoslovakia, Poland, and Hungary each be reduced to 275,000 military personnel. At present the United States deploys about 217,000 Army and 88,000 Air Force personnel in West Germany.[34] The Soviet Union is estimated to maintain (before any unilateral cuts by Gorbachev) stationed ground forces of 380,000 in East Germany, 80,000 in Czechoslovakia, 40,000 in Poland, and 65,000 in Hungary, for a total of 565,000 in the army. And there are probably 58,000 men, along with 4 tactical air armies, deployed in these countries.[35] If only U.S. and Soviet troops were at issue, that would mean a trade of 30,000 U.S. military personnel for 348,000 Soviet troops, one of the better deals in arms control history. To illustrate the implications of such a trade—based on proportionate cuts—Soviet ground forces would fall to 167,737 (or 8 division forces) in East Germany; to 35,313 in Czechoslovakia (or 1⅓ division forces); to 17,656 in Poland (1 small division force); and to 28,642 (or 1⅔ division forces) in Hungary—for a total of 12 divisions. The United States, for its part, would presumably dismantle 1 division and 1 fighter-attack wing.[36]

Soviet negotiators, however, have pointed out that Belgium, Britain, France, and the Netherlands also station more than 100,000 (perhaps as many as 147,000) military personnel in West Germany, and that these forces along with the U.S. total should be included in any reduction to a ceiling of 275,000. Should that argument be accepted, withdrawals from West Germany and other NATO countries would have to come to as many as 177,000 troops in all rather than the 30,000 proposed by President Bush. If these cuts were taken proportionately by all the NATO countries with troops stationed primarily in West Germany, the United States would be obligated to take out more than 119,000 military personnel. Measured in terms of units, that could mean a withdrawal of as many as 2⅓ division

34. James H. Webb, Jr., "For a Defense That Makes Sense," *New York Times Magazine*, May 21, 1989, p. 40.
35. See International Institute for Strategic Studies, *The Military Balance, 1988–1989* (Autumn 1988), pp. 48–52.
36. *New York Times*, May 29, 1989, pp. A1, A6, and May 30, 1989, p. A13.

forces and 3⅓ fighter-attack wings as well as the demobilization of the personnel and the destruction of their equipment.[37]

Savings resulting from these constraints would amount to $12.3 billion a year once the withdrawal, the demobilization, and the destruction of equipment had been completed. That amount, along with the annual saving of $1.4 billion on strategic nuclear forces, would bring national defense spending down to $251.3 billion by 1996 or 1997 (see table 28).

37. See table 25 for NATO and Warsaw Pact ground and fighter-attack forces in 1990 and after two stages of CFE reductions. See also Flora Lewis, "Beyond the Glue of Fear," *New York Times*, June 4, 1989, p. E31.

CHAPTER FOUR

DEFENSE AFTER START AND CFE AGREEMENTS, 1997–2000

IF THE START and CFE agreements are concluded, such a result need not and indeed should not mean the end of military reductions and budgets. Rather, the two agreements should be seen as the first important steps in what could be a continuing process. To take the case of the strategic nuclear forces, as the Soviet Union moves out of silos toward more land-mobile missiles, while the United States emphasizes submarine-launched ballistic missiles and cruise-missile-carrying bombers at the expense of ICBMs, the number of targetable aiming points will probably decline, as will the demand for coverage of such nonstrategic targets as tactical airfields and ground force bases. These developments should permit further cuts in warheads, launchers, and costs—though the issue of both the type and pace of any modernization of these capabilities will remain. Strategic systems will require replacement, and technology will advance in many areas. Controls on the use of new technology and the role of the defense industry in the process will, in such an era, have to be rethought.

What seems even more evident is that the constraints on both conventional and nuclear forces within ATTU, though they will increase stability, will leave both the United States and the Soviet Union with large and powerful forces outside the constrained area, together with the means to move them back into ATTU on relatively short notice. Even if the Warsaw Pact forces west of the Urals were cut to 1,350,000 men and just under 67 divisions, from a current total of 154 divisions, the Soviets would still retain perhaps as many as 57 divisions east of the Urals, primarily oriented toward China, but also toward Japan.[38] The United States, for its part, might retain as many as 15⅓ active-duty Army and Marine Corps divisions

38. Department of Defense, *Soviet Military Power, 1988*, (April 1988), p. 15.

and 11 National Guard and Reserve divisions outside ATTU, along with enough airlift and sealift to move them back to Europe at a fairly rapid pace, especially if pre-positioned equipment remains available in West Germany (see table 26). In these circumstances the United States might well wonder about those divisions east of the Urals, and the Soviet Union want to count the U.S. weapons held in storage in Western Europe, since there are enough of them to permit (at least in principle) the rapid reinforcement of NATO with four heavy divisions from the United States. Achieving stability in ATTU, therefore, and effectively requiring a long and very evident mobilization by any party wishing to upset the equilibrium, cannot be separated from a concern about other parts of the world and the forces outside ATTU held by the USSR and the United States. Indeed, unless measures are taken to place restraints on these other forces and their intercontinental mobility, doubts are bound to remain about the long-term efficacy of CFE. What is more, the pressures to retain substantial nuclear capabilities in ATTU as insurance against any conventional breakdown are likely to increase again.

1999: Case A

Dealing with the strategic nuclear balance is the lesser of the two challenges. It is a worldwide problem to begin with, and there are only two parties to the negotiations, although, as their arsenals decline, the United States may wish to include other nuclear powers in the discussion. One option for such future negotiations does not seem likely: the abolition of all nuclear weapons. Indeed, a regrettable reality of the times is that no way exists to get rid of nuclear weapons or, equally important, of the knowledge of how to manufacture and deliver them. The nuclear genie has been out of the bottle for a long time.

It is equally true that 13,000, or even 6,000, nuclear warheads may seem excessive for purposes of deterrence. Nonetheless, there is some floor below which relatively small but surreptitious changes in the number held by one side could create instabilities that would not be possible with larger forces. It would not much matter if one side has 5,000 survivable weapons and the other side 6,000. However, depending on other factors, it could be most troublesome if one side had only 200 and the other side managed to acquire 1,000 or more.

At present the United States and the Soviet Union are nowhere near levels that lend themselves to such a disequilibrium, and a START agreement with 6,000 "accountable" weapons on each side should prove equally stable. But how far could U.S. and Soviet strategic nuclear forces shrink and still retain the ability both to cover a comprehensive array of targets and to withhold attacks on some of them?

The answer greatly depends on how the United States and the Soviet Union reconfigure their forces after the START and CFE negotiations have concluded. Suppose, however, that the Soviets lower the throw-weight of their ICBMs and shift the missiles from silos to road or rail mobility and that they cut their conventional ground and tactical air forces roughly in half. These changes should have a strong effect on the number of aiming points of interest to the United States. Under such conditions the U.S. target list—even with a large urban-industrial component—could fall to fewer than 2,100 separate aiming points, assuming that only home bases for land-mobile missions would be targeted (see table 8). On the standard and demanding premise that the Soviet Union would strike first with only fifteen minutes of warning, and that U.S. capabilities would be caught on a day-to-day alert, an inventory of 4,056 warheads would be necessary to achieve a second-strike damage expectancy of 80 percent against the entire target list. Of the total inventory of warheads, 300 would be allocated to 100 Minuteman III ICBMs (with the Mark 12-A warhead), 492 to 41 B-1Bs equipped to carry ALCMs or ACMs (advanced cruise missiles), and 3,264 to 144 Trident I (C-4) and 264 Trident-II (D-5) SLBMs in a total of 17 submarines.[39] The surviving U.S. ICBMs and ALCMs, or ACMs, would be allocated to strategic targets in the USSR; Trident warheads could be withheld or used against any of the strategic, nonstrategic, economic, or urban targets as the national command authorities might determine.

The annual cost of this force would amount to $20.9 billion (see table 32). Such a budget would allow $12.7 billion a year for investment (procurement, RDT&E, and military construction) and $8.2 billion for operating, maintaining, and supporting the force. Besides the main offensive systems, these funds would also cover the costs of strategic surveillance, early warning, and communications capabilities, a continental defense of 180 active-duty fighters, tankers for refueling the bombers, and continued research on the strategic defense initiative at $3 billion a year. Savings from the START force would come to $6.8 billion a year. And without

39. See tables 32 and 9 for strategic nuclear forces, costs, and capabilities, 1990–99.

any further action, total outlays for national defense would fall to approximately $244.5 billion a year.[40]

It might well be preferable to make these reductions and savings by
means of a further agreement with the USSR. But because key elements
of the strategic nuclear forces would be highly survivable—regardless of
whether the Soviets reduced their offensive capabilities comparably—a
treaty would not be necessary unless the now well-established protocols
of arms control require equality and symmetry between the two sides and
continue to value them more highly than military stability. Admittedly the
U.S. retaliatory force looks small, with only 549 launchers, when the
Soviets might be free to retain 1,600 (see table 32). But the strategic
offense is conservatively designed: the triad is preserved, damage expectancy on a second strike would be high against a range of targets, and the
200 largest Soviet cities would remain at risk (see tables 8 and 9). In
addition, an active research and development program would guard against
the emergence of any serious vulnerabilities.

Furthermore, the strategic offense would be better balanced than it is
now. As currently constituted, the triad contains too many warheads that
have to be launched quickly and then wasted on strategic targets that are
unlikely to be of high value—indeed most of them would probably be
empty. By contrast, the smaller and cheaper force keeps fewer ICBMs
and bombers and depends heavily on more survivable and withholdable
SLBMs. As a result, the national command authorities have more options
and retain better control, including the ability to halt the exchange in a
matter of hours. At the same time they have the capability to prevent an
enemy from believing there is any conceivable advantage in starting a
nuclear exchange, no matter how cleverly it might allocate its forces. To
each of its moves the president, with this force, would have a countervailing move. The number of launchers may be small, but the number of
warheads would be larger than it was twenty years ago. Deterrence under
these conditions would be at least as well ensured.

To create a comparable situation with the conventional forces will be
difficult. Yet it may be possible to remove the more dangerous threats
and make any attempt to obtain a meaningful advantage in preparation
for a large-scale nonnuclear conflict costly, noisy, and time consuming.
Policymakers will also need to be alert to such changes.

40. This intermediate figure comes from subtracting $6.8 billion ($27.7 − $20.9) from the
1997 total of $251.3 billion.

Conceivably, the Soviet Union maintains 57 divisions east of the Urals primarily because of its long-standing differences with China and its apparent determination to cling to the four northern islands of Japan. However, a force of that size—even though distant from central Europe—is bound to foment suspicions about the stability of the military balance west of the Urals. Similarly, the Soviet Union is entitled to wonder about the size and purposes of the forces retained in the continental United States, along with the airlift and sealift and the power projection forces represented by the U.S. carrier battle groups and amphibious forces.

In the circumstances it would certainly be desirable to foster negotiations between the Soviet Union and China on what might constitute appropriate but lower levels of conventional forces in the Far East and press for a territorial settlement between the USSR and Japan, which could permit a further demobilization of Soviet forces. Resolution of these issues, along with continuation of what amounts to a military stalemate between North and South Korea—quite apart from any U.S. military presence in Korea and Okinawa—could then lead to a review of what conventional forces the United States might continue to need to maintain its overseas interests.

Such a review must begin by asking what kinds of military contingencies might confront the United States after the establishment of military stability in Europe and the Far East. It must also determine how many of these contingencies might affect U.S. interests and arise more or less simultaneously. Should Gorbachev gradually withdraw Soviet support for Cuba and Nicaragua, as seems not unlikely, the possible need for direct U.S. military intervention in Latin America would become increasingly remote, except perhaps in Panama. Southeast Asia will probably remain off limits to U.S. forces for some years to come and is clearly becoming more of a burden than an impoverished Vietnam can support without assistance from the Soviet Union, which no longer seems forthcoming. Only in the Middle East and Southwest Asia (including the Persian Gulf) are there both strong U.S. interests and the potential for a conflict serious enough to warrant American military intervention. It may also remain desirable to avoid giving Japan any excuse to add substantial military capabilities to its economic strength and influence. And the United States will certainly continue to insist on the maintenance of freedom of the seas and international airspace.

What this outlook suggests is that in the years immediately following the START and CFE negotiations the United States should prepare for

the rapid reinforcement of its remaining capabilities in Western Europe—
at least until the Soviets greatly reduce their forces east of the Urals. At
the same time it should retain enough ground and tactical air forces to
deal simultaneously with two relatively minor contingencies—each of
which might require a forced entry with amphibious forces and carrier
battle groups. And the Navy would almost certainly need the capabilities
to protect the sea-lanes to Europe and the Persian Gulf with major antisubmarine and anti–air warfare forces, unless and until an agreement can
be reached with the Soviet Union on naval limitations—an agreement that
the Soviets want and that could be in the U.S. interest.

Reinforcement of Europe, should it become necessary, would be pre-
ceded by considerable warning as a result of CFE. Consequently it could
become the responsibility of the 10 Army divisions and 12 Air Force
fighter-attack wings in the U.S. National Guard and Reserve. Mobility
would be provided by existing airlift and sealift. Forces for the two smaller
contingencies would consist of 4 active-duty Army, 3 active-duty Marine,
and 1 reserve Marine divisions, 34 AWACS (airborne warning and control
system) aircraft, 6 active Air Force and 3 active Marine fighter-attack
wings, the amphibious lift for 2 Marine brigades, and 9 carrier battle
groups. In addition, the Joint Chiefs of Staff would probably wish to
maintain the deployment of 1 Army brigade in Alaska and 1 in Panama,
along with 2 fighter-attack squadrons in each area. Control of two major
sea-lanes would probably claim 72 nuclear attack submarines, 260 P-3C
ASW (antisubmarine warfare) aircraft, the maintenance of SOSUS (sound
surveillance underwater system) CAPTOR mines, at least 3 destroyers
and 27 guided-missile frigates, along with various auxiliaries—including
ships that can tow arrays of sonobuoys to detect approaching submarines.
All such forces would also need a number of service and support aircraft.

Counting active-duty and reserve forces, as well as units remaining in
Germany, these capabilities in total would comprise 23 divisions (19 Army
and 4 Marine Corps), 27 fighter-attack wings (24 Air Force and 3 Marine
Corps), and 352 ships, submarines, and auxiliaries (excluding SSBNs and
their support ships, which are carried in the budget for the strategic nuclear
forces).[41] The annual cost of this capability would come to $123.5 billion
(see table 15). Total outlays for all forces, conventional, tactical nuclear,
and strategic nuclear, would add up to $147.9 billion. In addition, defense
would have to pay $26 billion for national intelligence and communications

41. See table 32 for conventional forces (case A) in fiscal 1999.

and $21 billion for retired pay accrual. The grand total for national defense would therefore come to $194.9 billion (see table 32).

1999: Case B

The costs of case A assume that the Soviet Union and China had not reached an agreement on mutual force reductions and that the United States and the USSR had not entered negotiations to limit their naval forces. Should those two eventualities come to pass, more cuts in U.S. defense outlays would become feasible. The first would reduce still further the threat to Europe and could produce corresponding changes on the U.S. side. The National Guard and Reserve is probably immune to abolition, however great the changes on the international scene. Even so, its personnel could be limited to a million, armored and mechanized divisions could be converted to lighter formations, and the Pentagon could reduce its funding of reserve investment and training, which would make these units even less threatening than they are now. Actions of this kind could save $5 billion a year.

As already indicated, verifiable measures could be taken to segregate TLAM-Ns from conventional SLCMs. A naval agreement could get rid of the nuclear versions on both sides and save the Pentagon another $1.5 billion a year. A further agreement to limit each side to 36 nuclear attack submarines for sea-lane protection (which would heighten the safety of the SSBNs on both sides) would save another $3.9 billion a year, yet would still leave the Navy with the capability to conduct ASW barrier operations in at least one major ocean.

All told, these further agreements could bring U.S. defense spending down another $10.4 billion to a total of $184.5 billion a year (see table 32).

1999: Case C

To allay alleged Soviet anxieties about U.S. aircraft carriers, and to take a slightly less conservative approach to minor contingencies, it should be possible to cut the total number of carrier battle groups to 6 (which would permit 4 to go on station in an emergency) and limit the number of active-duty divisions to 10 (7 Army and 3 Marine Corps), of which 6 would be available for special operations and low-intensity conflict. These reductions would save another $15.6 billion and bring annual defense spending down to $168.9 billion, approximately 56 percent of what it is now (see table 32).

Defense would be directed to maintain the strategic and tactical nuclear forces described in cases A and B, along with options for their use. Conventional forces would now be designed to

—maintain a hedge against any future Soviet threat to Europe with 3⅔ active Army divisions and 7⅓ active Air Force fighter-attack wings (in West Germany), along with 10 Army divisions and 12 Air Force fighter-attack wings from the National Guard (in the CONUS);

—program the forces for two relatively minor contingencies with a total of 6 carrier battle groups, the amphibious lift for 2 Marine Corps brigades, 6 divisions (2 active Army, 3 active Marine Corps, and 1 reserve Marine Corps), 2⅔ Air Force and 3 Marine Corps fighter-attack wings (or the equivalent of 8⅔ Air Force wings);

—keep 1⅓ active Army divisions and 2 active Air Force wings either as a Joint Chiefs of Staff reserve or for deployment to Alaska and, possibly, Panama.

Ground forces would consist of 21 divisions, supported by 15 fighter-attack wings and 257 Navy general purpose ships and submarines. Long-range mobility would be provided by 407 wide-bodied aircraft and 222 transport and cargo ships—unless agreement were reached to curtail government-owned aircraft and sealift.

1999: Case D

If these steps could be successfully taken, additional but modest adjustments would be in order. U.S. force structure would remain fixed. But SDI outlays would be reduced from $3 billion to $2.1 billion, and the program would become part of the technology base in research and development. The inventory of air-launched cruise missiles for the B-1B would also be reduced with the certification and deployment of the advanced cruise missile. At the same time, command, control, communications, and intelligence (previously frozen at about $26 billion) would be cut by 30 percent and retailored to function with the smaller U.S. forces. As a consequence, national defense spending would decline from $168.9 billion to $160.1 billion. Between 1990 and 1999, if these and all previous measures could be implemented, these same outlays would fall by nearly 47 percent (see table 32).

Conclusion

What is important to recognize, however, is not that some specific goal should be reached or that the numbers used here are precise indicators of what could be done. Instead, several key points are in need of greater recognition than they have received so far. First, a revolution in military affairs could be in the making at least in part because of the economic distress in the USSR and the changes in Soviet leadership. Granted the revolution may not go as far as has been suggested here. But one thing is clear: the revolution will not progress much further without initiatives from and cooperation by the United States. Second, caution may be in order for Washington, but not to the point of refusing to think about what would constitute a plausibly desirable future in the military realm, how we might get there, and what difference it would make to the defense establishment, defense industry, and research and development. Third, whatever else the United States may decide to do in aid of Gorbachev, it can collaborate with him to reallocate resources from the defense to the civil sector. That will probably help him more than any economic assistance the United States could or would provide. And, as Secretary of State James A. Baker III has pointed out, agreements on arms reductions could have a longer-term effect even if Gorbachev fell from office.

Admittedly, the path projected here could have many twists and turns, and the end does not promise all sweetness and light. Canada, West Germany, France, Italy, Japan, the United Kingdom, and the United States are already making efforts to prevent the proliferation of missiles and chemical weapons as well as nuclear weapons. But potential belligerents such as North and South Korea, India and Pakistan, Iran and Iraq, Syria and Israel—among others—continue to maintain or seek to acquire these capabilities.[42] Regional conflicts affecting U.S. interests are likely to continue in Africa, the Middle East, Southwest Asia, and Latin America. Nuclear forces of some magnitude will continue to exist.

Despite these and other dangers, it may be well to recall that U.S. and Soviet nuclear forces have grown three times larger (measured in war-

42. See David Silverberg, *Defense News*, September 4, 1989, pp. 30–32, 34.

heads) than a conservative policy of deterrence would require, and that each capability costs nearly $30 billion more than necessary because of a competition that is going nowhere. It is also of some relevance that the conventional defense of Western Europe now costs the United States about $126 billion a year, of which no more than $22 billion has to do with maintaining a significant U.S. presence in Europe with 3⅔ divisions and 7⅓ fighter-attack wings.

To put the matter another way, if retired pay accrual were removed from U.S. defense expenditures for 1990, approximately 50 percent of the remainder (or $140 billion) would result from the military competition with the Soviet Union. Cumulatively, the United States could save more than $500 billion during the coming decade if the military competition were replaced by a cooperative reduction of armaments.

Now that the Soviet leadership has recognized how much it has suffered from the competition, at least for now, and how high the cost has proved, an opportunity presents itself to put an end to the military contest and to the risks that have accompanied it. This study is one view of how to halt the competition and one effort to spell out the implications of such a process for U.S. defense programs and budgets during the coming decade.[43] These implications appear to be substantial. The time has come to start working them out now, whether on this basis or on some other.

43. For a summary of changes in forces and costs, from 1990 to 1999 (case D), see table 32.

CHAPTER FIVE

SUMMARY OF PROPOSED REDUCTIONS

THE UNITED STATES has not yet adjusted its national defense spending plans to deal with the evolving conditions in the Soviet Union and Eastern Europe. Such an adjustment is essential for many reasons. The Soviet Union has already begun to reduce its conventional forces (as have other members of the Warsaw Pact). Furthermore, Moscow is now willing to accept parity at reduced levels in nuclear forces with the United States and conventional capabilities with NATO. The United States, for its part, has strong domestic incentives to reduce defense spending. It also has a stake both in ending the cold war and in furthering economic and political change in the communist bloc. Indeed, it can best encourage that change by facilitating a transfer of Warsaw Pact resources from military to civilian purposes, even if the process lasts no more than a decade and even if Gorbachev falls from power.

The essence of a revised defense spending plan would be to cooperate in ending the military competition with the Soviet Union and in reducing the resources devoted to defense by both sides. Such a process would necessarily involve several stages, during each of which the United States would hedge against both a breakdown of the process and crises in other parts of the world, and would move on to the next stage only if the previous one had been completed.

A *first stage* might run from 1990 to 1994. The Soviet leadership claims to have held its defense spending to zero growth since 1987, and it proposes to reduce defense by a minimum of 14.2 percent by 1991, with additional cuts to follow. The United States has already reduced defense budget authority by more than 13 percent since 1985, although outlays did not peak until 1987 and have fallen by only 6.4 percent since then. Despite these reductions, a good deal more can be taken out of national defense without any damage to current defense commitments. A first step in this direction would be to halt the rush to produce a next generation of weapons that is now in the acquisition pipeline—at a cumulative cost of more than

$117 billion[44]—and to delete the $48 billion in cumulative real growth planned by the Bush administration between 1990 and 1994. Total increases of $168.5 billion would be canceled as a result of

Cuts in	*Cumulative reduction, 1990–94 (billions)*
Major procurement	79.2
Minor procurement	34.7
Military personnel (62,500 active; 35,000 reserve)	16.7
Research, development, test, and evaluation	37.9
Total reduction	168.5

A second step between 1990 and 1994 would reduce national defense outlays from $300 billion to $265 billion for a cumulative saving of nearly $89 billion. This reduction would result in the removal of redundant forces and the segregation of the nuclear Tomahawk (TLAM-N) from conventional SLCMs. As a consequence, there would be

Cuts in	*Annual reduction, by 1994 (billions)*
Strategic nuclear forces (5,540 warheads and SDI)	22.9
Army active and reserve forces (1 active division and several reserve components)	3.6
Carrier battle groups (2)	5.9
Amphibious forces (ships for a fourth brigade)	2.1
Airlift capability (substitution of 15 C-5Bs for the C-17A)	2.0
Subtotal	36.5
Addition of	
10 cruise missile nuclear submarines (converted Poseidon boats)	− 1.5
Total reduction	35.0

A second stage would probably overlap with the first and might end in 1997. It would be marked by completion and implementation of the START and conventional forces in Europe (CFE) treaties. Assuming their full implementation, national defense outlays would fall from $265 billion to $251.3 billion. The reduction of $13.7 billion would come from

---

44. All dollar amounts are in 1990 dollars.

Cuts in	Annual reduction by 1997 (billions)
Strategic nuclear forces (597 warheads)	1.4
Army active forces (2⅓ divisions withdrawn from Europe and demobilized)	8.0
Air Force active aircraft (240 combat aircraft withdrawn from Europe and destroyed)	4.3
Total reduction	13.7

START would increase strategic nuclear stability, and CFE would reduce the probability of surprise attack and increase the time needed to put together a major attack with conventional forces in Europe west of the Urals. However, under START both parties would still have an excess of strategic offensive forces in light of increased missile mobility and a decline in the number of critical targets that either side could cover. CFE would also be limited in its effects. It would not cover naval forces, and it would not constrain Soviet forces east of the Urals or U.S. forces outside Western Europe. Presumably, both the United States and the Soviet Union would have incentives to bring these other forces within the arms control and reduction regime.

Consequently, *a third stage* in the process could be visualized by the and of the century. Such a stage might consist of a sequence of four steps. The first would entail agreements to: (a) reduce strategic offensive forces to approximately 4,100 warheads; (b) cut Soviet conventional forces east of the Urals by at least 9 Category I divisions and 416 combat aircraft and reduce comparable U.S. forces in the CONUS; and (c) trade U.S. carrier battle groups for Soviet nuclear attack submarines. As a result of these agreements, U.S. defense spending would decline from $251.3 billion to $194.9 billion. The reduction of $56.4 billion would result from

Cuts in	Annual reduction by 1999 (billions)
Strategic nuclear warheads (2,387 warheads)	6.8
Army active forces (6⅔ divisions in the CONUS)	22.8
Air Force active forces (624 combat aircraft in the CONUS)	11.0
Navy carriers (3 carrier battle groups—63 ships)	8.8
Amphibious forces (the lift for 1 Marine Corps brigade)	2.1
Antisubmarine warfare forces (64 surface combatants and auxiliaries)	4.9
Total reduction	56.4

The second step would require further agreements with the Soviet Union to: (a) abolish all long-range nuclear cruise missiles; and (b) reduce both U.S. and Soviet attack submarines so as to increase the survivability of the SSBNs (nuclear ballistic missile submarines) and minimize the threat to the main sea lines of communication. Because of previous treaties lengthening the time in which the Soviet Union could develop any conventional threat to Europe, China, or Japan, the United States would also limit the procurement and operation and maintenance (O&M) accounts of the Army National Guard and Reserve in order to reduce their readiness to that of Soviet Category III divisions. National defense spending would fall from $194.9 billion to $184.5 billion. The reduction of $10.4 billion would come specifically from

Cuts in	*Annual reduction by 1999 (billions)*
Tactical nuclear forces (10 nuclear guided missile submarines with 700 TLAM-N)	1.5
Nuclear attack submarines (36 boats)	3.9
Army National Guard and Reserve (O&M and procurement accounts)	5.0
Total reduction	10.4

A third step would entail a revision of U.S. force planning assumptions. Defense would be instructed to maintain existing strategic and tactical nuclear forces, along with options for their use. Conventional forces would be designed to do the following:

a. Maintain a hedge against a Soviet threat to Europe with 3⅔ active Army divisions and 7⅓ active Air Force wings (in West Germany) and 10 Army divisions and 12 Air Force fighter-attack wings from the National Guard (in the CONUS).

b. Program the forces for two relatively minor contingencies with a total of

—6 carrier battle groups

—the amphibious lift for 2 Marine Corps brigades

—6 divisions (2 active Army, 3 active and 1 reserve Marine Corps)

—2⅔ Air Force and 3 Marine Corps fighter-attack wings (or the equivalent of 8⅔ Air Force wings).

c. Hold as a Joint Chiefs reserve or for deployment to Alaska and Panama

—1⅓ active Army division

—2 active Air Force wings.

The total number of divisions would consist of 21, supported by 15 fighter-attack wings and 257 Navy ships and submarines. Long-range mobility would be provided by 407 wide-bodied aircraft and 222 transport and cargo ships. With this strategic concept, national defense spending would decline from $184.5 billion to $168.9 billion. The reduction of $15.6 billion would result from

Cuts in	*Annual reduction by 1999 (billions)*
Army active forces (2 divisions)	6.8
Navy active forces (3 carrier battle groups)	8.8
Total reduction	15.6

A fourth step would avoid making any further changes in force structure. However, the strategic defense initiative would be reduced in funding and become part of the technology base in research and development. The inventory of air-launched cruise missiles for the B-1B would be reduced with the certification and deployment of the advanced cruise missile. And command, control, and communications (previously untouched) would be retailored to function with the smaller forces. National defense spending would decline from $168.9 billion to $160.1 billion. The reduction of $8.8 billion would result from

Cuts in	*Annual reduction by 1999 (billions)*
Air-launched cruise missiles (154)	0.1
SDI	0.9
Command, control, and communications	7.8
Total reduction	8.8

Further detail on the reductions between 1990 and 1999 is shown in the tables.

TABLES

Table 1. U.S. National Defense Outlays, Fiscal Years 1930–90
Billions of 1990 dollars

Year	Outlays	Year	Outlays	Year	Outlays
1930	11.4	1950	105.9	1970	289.8
1931	11.4	1951	166.7	1971	262.7
1932	11.8	1952	299.6	1972	243.6
1933	10.2	1953	330.8	1973	221.1
1934	7.5	1954	314.9	1974	211.2
1935	10.2	1955	268.7	1975	209.9
1936	12.4	1956	254.6	1976	203.3
1937	12.4	1957	258.6	1977	206.4
1938	13.5	1958	252.8	1978	207.3
1939	14.0	1959	254.0	1979	215.0
1940	22.2	1960	248.0	1980	221.0
1941	73.4	1961	248.8	1981	231.6
1942	248.3	1962	261.5	1982	250.7
1943	594.7	1963	265.3	1983	271.8
1944	725.7	1964	261.7	1984	284.9
1945	803.9	1965	236.7	1985	306.6
1946	415.7	1966	255.2	1986	308.6
1947	113.6	1967	296.5	1987	319.3
1948	77.8	1968	323.7	1988	314.4
1949	107.4	1969	314.5	1989	310.2
				1990	300.0

Sources: U.S. Bureau of the Census, *Historical Statistics of the United States, Colonial Times to 1970*, pts. 1 and 2 (1975), pp. 230, 1115–16; *Historical Tables, Budget of the United States Government, Fiscal Year 1986*, pp. 6.1(1)–6.1(8); and *Department of Defense Annual Report, Fiscal Year 1986*, p. 78, *Fiscal Year 1988*, p. 86, and *Fiscal Year 1990*, p. 83.

Table 2. CIA Estimates of Soviet Defense Spending and Defense as a Percent of GNP, 1955–82, plus Extrapolations, 1983–89

Outlays in billions of 1970 rubles

Year	Outlays	Percent of GNP	Year	Outlays	Percent of GNP
1955	30	17	1973	53	12
1956	29	15	1974	57	13
1957	26	13	1975	59	13
1958	26	12	1976	63	13
1959	26	11	1977	63	13
1960	27	12	1978	64	13
1961	30	12	1979	66	13
1962	34	13	1980	67	14
1963	35	14	1981	68	13–14
1964	38	14	1982	70	13–14
1965	39	13	*Extrapolations*[a]		
1966	40	13	1983	71	14
1967	43	13	1984	73	14
1968	46	13	1985	74	14
1969	48	13	1986	76	14
1970	49	13	1987	78	14–15
1971	50	12	1988	78	14–15
1972	51	13	1989	78	14–15

Sources: Abraham S. Becker, *Sitting on Bayonets: The Soviet Defense Burden and the Slowdown of Soviet Defense Spending*, JRS-01 (RAND-UCLA Center for the Study of Soviet International Behavior, December 1985), pp. 4, 13; and author's estimates.

a. Based on a 2 percent real growth between 1976 and 1987, and zero real growth since 1987, as announced by Gorbachev. *New York Times*, May 31, 1989, p. A10.

Table 3. Proposed Reductions in National Defense Outlays, Fiscal Years 1990–94
Billions of 1990 dollars

Outlays	1990	1991	1992	1993	1994	1990–94
Inherited five-year defense program (FYDP)	314.5	326.2	337.5	341.9	350.2	1,688.5[a]
Cheney FYDP	300.0	305.5	307.7	313.8	321.0	1,548.0
Reduction	14.5	20.7	28.0	28.1	29.2	120.5
Cheney FYDP	300.0	305.5	307.7	313.8	321.0	1,548.0
Zero real growth	300.0	300.0	300.0	300.0	300.0	1,500.0
Reduction	. . .	5.5	7.7	13.8	21.0	48.0
Combined reduction	14.5	26.2	35.7	41.9	50.2	168.5
Zero real growth	300.0	300.0	300.0	300.0	300.0	1,500.0
Reduced FYDP	300.0	291.5	282.7	274.1	265.0	1,413.3
Reduction	. . .	8.5	17.3	25.9	35.0	86.7
Actual saving	. . .	14.0	25.0	39.7	56.0	134.7
Hypothetical saving	9.5	21.9	47.2	73.2	100.6	252.4

Source: Author's estimates based on *Department of Defense Annual Report, Fiscal 1988*, p. 98; *Fiscal 1990*, pp. 89, 219; and *Budget of the United States Government, Fiscal Year 1990*, p. 5-15.

a. These outlays reflect the cost of continuing at its planned pace the program inherited by Secretary of Defense Richard Cheney.

/

Table 4. Reductions in Outlays for Major Procurement, Fiscal Years 1990–94[a]
Millions of 1990 dollars

Item	1990	1991	1992	1993	1994	Total
Army						
AHIP (Army helicopter improvement program)	45.8	180.0	267.4	318.5	336.8	...
ATACMS (Army tactical missile system)	10.7	71.0	138.2	177.9	194.7	...
FAADS C² (Forward area air defense system, command control)	3.1	26.1	72.3	147.9	225.4	...
FAADS LOS-F-H (line of sight-forward heavy)	32.6	202.6	333.9	394.5	436.0	...
FAADS LOS-R (line of sight-rear)	9.4	60.5	109.0	133.8	134.9	...
FAADS FOG-M (fiber optic guided missile)	2.5	23.0	78.6	158.4	283.3	...
Navy						
D-5 (Trident II) missile	...	1,050.0	1,000.0	950.0	900.0	...
F-14D Navy fighter aircraft	110.5	565.8	1,007.9	1,479.2	2,029.5	...
LRAACA (long-range air ASW capability aircraft)	...	1.8	41.5	201.7	421.4	...
V-22 tilt-rotor aircraft	129.4	668.9	1,223.0	1,674.1	1,953.0	...
CV SLEP (career service life improvement program)	34.9	...	...	204.3	294.3	...
DDG-51 guided-missile destroyer	188.1	739.7	1,478.0	2,122.8	2,784.7	...
LCAC (landing craft air cushion)	...	...	...	157.1	208.6	...
LHD-1 amphibious ship	...	...	...	221.4	367.9	...
LSD-41 variant amphibious ship	11.9	47.0	93.8	136.5	185.5	...

SSN-21 nuclear attack submarine	42.7	286.7	809.7	1,469.9	2,143.3	...
AMRAAM (advanced medium-range air-to-air missile)	14.5	88.7	233.6	334.6	386.5	...
Air Force						
B-1B bomber	...	4.5	17.5	80.6	140.5	...
B-2 Stealth bomber	3,200.0	3,750.0	4,300.0	2,650.0	3,533.0	...
C-17A long-range cargo aircraft	130.6	939.3	1,877.0	2,964.5	3,715.6	...
F-15E fighter-attack aircraft	103.7	710.6	1,167.1	1,372.3	1,399.8	...
KC-135R tanker	...	...	292.0	365.1	475.5	...
V-22 tilt-rotor aircraft	...	...	24.3	296.7	557.3	...
AMRAAM (advanced medium-range air-to-air missile)	228.7	506.2	636.3	610.9	578.2	...
MX ICBM	281.3	585.7	715.7	687.2	656.7	...
Rail garrison (train-mobile)	55.4	389.1	703.0	824.9	618.3	...
SRAM II (short-range attack missile)	...	24.0	59.8	123.2	185.3	...
Tacit Rainbow radar-seeking missile	...	48.2	82.2	109.4	119.9	...
JSTARS (joint surveillance and target attack radar system)	...	27.2	148.4	342.8	738.6	...
Summary						
Army	104.1	563.2	999.4	1,331.0	1,611.0	4,608.8
Navy	532.0	3,448.6	5,887.5	8,951.6	11,675.2	30,494.9
Air Force	3,999.7	6,984.8	10,023.3	10,427.6	12,718.7	44,154.1
Total	4,635.8	10,996.6	16,910.2	20,710.2	26,005.0	79,257.8

Sources: Congressional Budget Office, April 17, 1989; and author's estimates.

a. These reductions are taken to help remove the backlog of programs that would otherwise increase national defense spending by at least 5 percent a year, in real terms, between fiscal 1990 and 1994. See table 3.

Table 5. Reductions in National Defense Outlays for Research, Development, Test, and Evaluation, Fiscal Years 1990–94[a]

Millions of 1990 dollars

Item	1990	1991	1992	1993	1994	Total
Small ICBM (transporter-mobile)	. . .	100.0	200.0	300.0	400.0	1,000.0
Rail garrison (train-mobile)	63.2	543.8	357.3	152.5	40.9	1,157.7
B-2 Stealth bomber	1,000.0	1,000.0	1,000.0	1,000.0	1,000.0	5,000.0
SRAM II (short-range attack missile)	115.0	184.0	178.4	84.6	21.1	583.1
Strategic defense initiative	1,600.0	2,400.0	3,200.0	4,100.0	5,200.0	16,500.0
Air defense initiative	100.0	200.0	300.0	300.0	300.0	1,200.0
F-14sD Navy fighter	88.3	125.1	115.9	67.3	33.3	429.9
LRAACA (long-range air ASW capability aircraft)	106.7	196.3	192.5	157.5	109.8	762.8
V-22 (Navy) tilt-rotor aircraft	115.0	165.1	120.1	48.6	9.2	458.0
SSN-21 nuclear attack submarine	116.7	192.6	185.3	163.7	144.2	802.5
ATF (advanced tactical fighter)	642.7	1,263.1	1,579.1	2,055.3	2,037.3	7,557.5
C-17A long-range cargo aircraft	505.8	582.0	478.2	275.6	92.3	1,933.9
F-15E fighter-attack aircraft	66.0	95.1	69.8	42.5	29.0	302.4
V-22 (Air Force)	11.8	19.2	26.6	18.8	14.1	90.5
AMRAAM (advanced medium-range air-to-air missile)	11.9	18.1	25.0	27.6	28.0	110.6
Total	4,543.1	7,084.4	8,028.2	8,794.0	9,459.2	37,908.9

Sources: Congressional Budget Office, April 17, 1989; and author's estimates.

a. These reductions are taken to help remove the backlog of programs that would otherwise increase national defense spending by at least 5 percent a year, in real terms, between fiscal 1990 and 1994. See table 3.

Table 6. Estimates of Balance of National Defense Prior-Year Budget Authority, Fiscal Years 1988–90

Millions of current dollars

Budget authority	Start of 1988	End of 1988	End of 1989	End of 1990
Defense (051)[a]				
Obligated	212,484	216,941	218,376	227,721
Unobligated	47,621	42,292	41,196	43,614
Total	260,105	259,233	259,572	271,335
Energy				
Obligated	7,192	6,923	7,819	8,076
Unobligated	1,957	1,785	1,091	1,352
Total	9,194	8,708	8,910	9,428

Source: *Budget of the United States Government, Fiscal Year 1990*, p. 10-18.

a. The 051 account covers the funds of the Department of Defense; the 050 account (national defense) covers the military applications of atomic energy and several lesser functions as well as Department of Defense funds.

Table 7. U.S. Strategic Nuclear Forces and Costs, Selected Fiscal Years, 1990–99
Outlays in billions of 1990 dollars

Force type	Cheney, 1990		Reduced FYDP, 1994		START limits, 1997		Post-START limits, 1999 (Case D)	
	Number	Outlays	Number	Outlays	Number	Outlays	Number	Outlays
B-1B bomber	90	5.4	90	5.4	90	5.4	41	2.5
B-2 Stealth bomber	13	1.4	...	...	...	...	...	...
B-52G bomber	77	3.1	...	...	...	...	...	...
B-52H bomber	96	3.8	...	...	...	...	...	...
Air-launched cruise missile/short-range attack missile	4,000	2.6	1,846	1.2	1,846	1.2	492	0.3
KC-135R tanker	640	6.4	180	1.8	180	1.8	80	0.8
F-15 fighter	54	0.4	39	0.2	39	0.2	39	0.2
F-16 fighter	195	0.8	141	0.5	141	0.5	141	0.5
Minuteman II ICBM	450	2.1	...	...	...	...	...	...
Minuteman III ICBM	500	3.0	342	2.1	289	1.7	100	0.6
MX ICBM	50	2.3	...	...	...	...	...	...
Poseidon/C-3 SLBM[a]	176(16)	3.0	...	...	...	...	...	...
Poseidon/C-4 SLBM[a]	192(12)	3.8	144(9)	2.8	16(1)	0.1	...	...
Trident/C-4 SLBM[a]	240(10)	4.7	192(8)	3.8	192(8)	3.8	144(6)	2.9
Trident/D-5 SLBM[a]	...	...	192(8)	4.5	264(11)	6.2	264(11)	6.2
Early warning, surveillance, c³	...	3.8	...	3.8	...	3.8	...	3.8
Strategic defense initiative	...	5.4	...	3.0	...	3.0	...	2.1
Total annual outlays	...	52.0	...	29.1	...	27.7	...	19.9
Total offensive launchers	1,884.0	...	960	...	851	...	549	...

Sources: *Department of Defense Annual Report, Fiscal 1990*, p. 231; and author's estimates.
a. Numbers without parentheses are launchers; numbers in parentheses are submarines.

Table 8. Lists of Targets in the Soviet Union, Selected Fiscal Years, 1990–99

Type of target	1990	1994	1997	1999
Strategic forces				
Hard[a]	2,000	700	454	154
Soft[b]	650	650	150	150
Peripheral attack forces				
Missiles	50	. . .	. . .	. . .
Bomber bases	80	80	80	80
General purpose forces				
Ground force bases	300	300	100	50
Air force bases	150	150	100	50
Naval bases	20	20	20	10
Economic targets outside cities				
Transportation	300	300	300	100
Energy	200	200	200	100
Urban-industrial targets	1,380	1,380	1,380	1,380
Total	5,130	3,780	2,784	2,074

Source: Author's estimates.
a. Targets include silos, nuclear storage sites, and command centers.
b. Targets include strategic bomber bases, bases for land-mobile missiles, and land-mobile missiles.

Table 9. Capabilities of the U.S. Strategic Retaliatory Forces, Selected Fiscal Years 1990–99

Item	Cheney, 1990 Warhead inventory	Deliverable warheads[a]	Reduced FYDP, 1994 Warhead inventory	Deliverable warheads[a]	START limits 1997 Warhead inventory	Deliverable warheads[a]	Post-START limits, 1999 Warhead inventory	Deliverable warheads[a]
B-1B	1,800	346	1,800	392	1,800	392	492	116
B-52G	1,386	299	...	...	...	...	...	...
B-52H	1,728	373	...	...	...	...	...	...
Minuteman II	450	13	...	...	...	...	...	...
Minuteman III	1,500	43	1,026	30	867	25	300	9
MX	500	14	...	...	...	...	...	...
Poseidon/C-3	1,760	697	...	...	...	...	...	...
Poseidon/C-4	1,536	719	1,152	539	128	60	...	...
Trident/C-4	1,920	899	1,536	719	1,538	719	1,152	539
Trident/D-5	...	...	1,536	719	2,112	988	2,112	988
Total	12,580	3,403	7,050	2,399	6,443	2,184	4,056	1,652
Accountable warheads								
Bombers	3,158		1,080		1,080		492	
ICBMs	2,450		1,026		867		300	
SLBMs	5,216		4,224		3,776		3,264	
Total	10,822		6,330		5,723		4,056	
Percent of targets coverable								
Specified target list (table 8)	66		63		78		8	
Constant target list (5,130)	66		47		43		32	
Annual cost per deliverable warhead (millions of dollars)	11.8		9.0		8.5		8.1	

Sources: Tables 7 and 8; and author's estimates.

a. Deliverable after a well-executed Soviet first strike that gives fifteen minutes of response time; alert bombers (30 percent), 4 percent of alert ICBMs, and alert, on-station SLBMs survive. Only these launchers are assumed to be available for retaliation.

Table 10. U.S. Stockpile of Tactical Nuclear Weapons, 1983

Type of weapon	In the United States	In Europe		In the Pacific area	At sea	Total
		For U.S. forces	For non-U.S. forces			
Land based						
Aircraft bombs	1,210	1,415	320	135	. . .	3,080
Pershing I missiles	. . .	195[a]	100[a]	. . .	. . .	295
8-inch howitzers	200	505	430	65	. . .	1,200
155-mm howitzers	160	595	140	30	. . .	925
Lance missiles	210	325	370	. . .	. . .	905
Honest John rockets	100	. . .	200	. . .	. . .	300
Nike-Hercules surface-to-air missiles	55	300	390	. . .	. . .	745
Atomic demolition munitions	215	370	. . .	20	. . .	605
Naval						
Aircraft bombs	. . .	. . .	. . .	. . .	720	720
Depth charges	560	190	. . .	100	45	895
Terrier surface-to-air missiles	155	. . .	. . .	. . .	135	290
Antisubmarine rockets	225	. . .	. . .	. . .	350	575
Submarine rockets	110	. . .	. . .	. . .	175	285
Total	3,200	3,895[b]	1,950[b]	350	1,425	10,820

Source: Richard Halloran, "Report to Congress Provides Figures for Nuclear Arsenal," *New York Times*, November 15, 1983.
a. These warheads have been removed as a result of the Intermediate-range Nuclear Forces Treaty.
b. Approximately 1,400 of these weapons have been or will be withdrawn from Europe.

Table 11. U.S. National Defense Outlays for Tactical Nuclear Forces, Fiscal Years 1990, 1994

Billions of 1990 dollars

Item	Annual outlays
2,125 nuclear shells for artillery	0.2
3,080 nuclear bombs for tactical aircraft	0.3
905 nuclear warheads for Lance missiles	0.6
758 Tomahawk nuclear land-attack missiles (TLAM-N)	0.9
Total in fiscal 1990	2.0
10 nuclear cruise missile submarines (SSGN)	1.5
Total in fiscal 1994	3.5

Sources: Table 10; and author's estimates.

Table 12. U.S. National Defense Outlays by Force Planning Contingencies, Fiscal Years 1990, 1999

Billions of 1990 dollars

Force planning contingency	Cheney, 1990	1999 (case D)
Strategic nuclear deterrence	52.0	19.9
Tactical nuclear deterrence	2.0	2.0
Conventional defense of		
Central Europe	74.9	34.8
North Norway	16.1	. . .
Mediterranean	9.1	. . .
Atlantic sea-lanes	23.9	5.3
Persian Gulf	19.4	21.4
Indian ocean sea-lanes	a	a
South Korea	12.0	. . .
Pacific sea-lanes	20.1	5.2
Alaska	3.6	3.6
Panama	3.6	3.6
Latin America	7.5	19.3
Continental United States	8.8	5.8
National intelligence and communications	26.0	18.2
Retired pay accrual	21.0	21.0
Total	300.0	160.1

Source: Author's estimates.
a. Less than $50 million.

Table 13. Published Soviet Defense Outlays, 1989

Billions of rubles

Item	Outlays
Operations[a]	20.2
Procurement	32.6
Construction	4.6
Military research and development	15.3
Military space programs	3.9
Military pensions	2.3
Other military	2.3
Total	81.2[b]

Sources: Gur Ofer, "Fiscal and Monetary Aspects of Soviet Economic Reform," paper presented at the Ninth Latin American Meeting of the Econometric Society, Santiago, Chile, August 1-3, 1989; and *Washington Post*, June 8, 1989, pp. A25, 27.

a. The *Washington Post* labels this item as salaries to armed forces personnel. If that is correct, outlays for operation and maintenance are missing.

b. According to the *New York Times*, May 31, 1989, p. A10, CIA estimates Soviet defense outlays at between 115 and 125 billion rubles.

Table 14. U.S. Military and Civilian Personnel, Selected Fiscal Years, 1990–99
Thousands of people

Item	Cheney, 1990	Reduced forces		1990			
		1994	1997	Case A	Case B	Case C	Case D
Military personnel (active duty)							
Army	764.4	701.6	636.1	439.6	374.3	370.7	370.7
Navy	543.4	543.4	528.0	470.0	466.1	365.8	352.8
Marine Corps	197.2	197.0	197.0	197.0	197.0	197.0	197.0
Air Force	567.9	521.2	504.4	394.8	432.3	428.1	420.0
Total	2,121.5[a]	1,963.2	1,865.5	1,501.4	1,469.7	1,361.6	1,340.5
Civilian personnel (direct hire)	1,019.6	1,021.3	970.5	781.1	764.6	708.4	697.4
National Guard and Reserve							
Army	779.7	772.0	772.0	772.0	772.0	772.0	772.0
Navy	153.4	149.0	149.0	149.0	149.0	149.0	149.0
Marine Corps	44.0	43.0	43.0	43.0	43.0	43.0	43.0
Air Force	201.1	193.0	193.0	193.0	193.0	193.0	193.0
Total	1,178.2[a]	1,157.0	1,157.0	1,157.0	1,157.0	1,157.0	1,157.0

Sources: *Department of Defense Annual Report, Fiscal Year 1990*, p. 226; and author's estimates.
a. These totals are reductions of 62,500 in active-duty and 34,800 in reserve personnel from the strengths planned in 1988. See *Department of Defense Annual Report, Fiscal Year 1988*, p. 334.

Table 15. U.S. National Defense Outlays, Conventional Forces, Selected Fiscal Years, 1990–99
Billions of fiscal 1990 dollars

Functions	Cheney, 1990	Reduced FYDP, 1994	START, CFE, 1997	After START and CFE, 1999			
				Case A	Case B	Case C	Case D
Army divisions							
Active duty	64.9	61.5	53.5	30.7	30.7	23.9	23.9
Reserve	10. 0	9.8	9.8	9.8	4.8	4.8	4.8
Marine divisions							
Active duty	3.8	3.8	3.8	3.8	3.8	3.8	3.8
Reserve	0.5	0.5	0.5	0.5	0.5	0.5	0.5
Marine tactical aircraft	4.2	4.2	4.2	4.2	4.2	4.2	4.2
Air Force tactical aircraft							
Active duty	30.8	30.8	26.5	15.5	15.5	15.5	15.5
Reserve	5.0	5.0	5.0	5.0	5.0	5.0	5.0
Navy							
Carrier battle groups	41.1	35.2	35.2	26.4	26.4	17.6	17.6
Amphibious groups	8.4	6.3	6.3	4.2	4.2	4.2	4.2
Antisubmarine warfare	19.3	19.3	19.3	14.4	10.5	10.5	10.5
Airlift and sealift	11.0	9.0	9.0	9.0	9.0	9.0	9.0
Total	199.0	185.4	173.1	123.5	114.6	99.0	99.0

Source: Author's estimates.

Table 16. U.S. National Defense Outlays for Major Procurement, Fiscal Years 1990–94
Billions of 1990 dollars

Capability	Outlays
Strategic nuclear forces	31.7
Tactical nuclear forces	2.5
Land forces (Army and Marine Corps)	39.2
Land-based tactical air forces (Air Force and Marine Corps)	42.0
Navy aircraft and ships	68.0
Airlift and sealift	7.4
National intelligence and communications	26.9
Total	217.7

Sources: Tables 7, 11, and 15; and author's estimates.

Table 17. U.S. National Defense Outlays for Other Procurement, by Object Class, Selected Fiscal Years, 1990–99
Billions of 1990 dollars

Object class	Cheney, 1990	Reduced FYDP			START, CFE, 1997	1999			
		1991	1992	1993	1994		Case A	Case B	Case C	Case D
Aircraft modifications	4.0	3.8	3.7	3.6	3.5	3.2	2.5	2.2	2.0	1.8
Aircraft spares	4.7	4.6	4.5	4.3	4.2	3.9	3.0	2.7	2.5	2.2
Support equipment and vehicles	7.3	7.0	6.8	6.6	6.4	6.0	4.6	4.1	3.7	3.4
Communications and electronics	5.6	5.5	5.2	5.1	4.8	4.6	3.5	3.2	2.9	2.7
Ammunition	4.2	4.0	3.9	3.7	3.6	3.4	2.6	2.3	2.1	1.9
Tactical missiles	4.2	4.1	4.0	3.8	3.7	3.5	2.6	2.4	2.2	2.0
Miscellaneous equipment	3.6	3.6	3.4	3.4	3.2	3.2	3.2	2.2	1.9	1.9
Total	33.6	32.6	31.5	30.5	29.4	27.8	21.0	19.1	17.3	15.9

Sources: Author's estimates.

Table 18. U.S. Outlays for Major Procurement by Weapons and Equipment, Fiscal Years 1990–94

Billions of 1990 dollars

Item	Number	Outlays
Strategic nuclear forces		
B-1B bomber conversion (to cruise missile carrier)	90	0.8
Advanced cruise missile	1,080	7.8
Rotary launchers	26	0.1
KC-135 refueling aircraft	126	1.6
Minuteman III upgrades	300	2.4
Trident II submarine	5	8.9
D-5 (Trident II) ballistic missile	175	6.5
Defense support program satellites	6	3.6
Tactical nuclear forces		
Conversion of Poseidon SSBMs to SSGNs	5	1.5
TLAM-N (Tomahawk land-attack missile, nuclear)	165	1.0
Conventional forces		
Tanks (Army and Marine Corps)	3,175	11.3
Other tracked vehicles (Army and Marine Corps)	4,150	4.6
Helicopters (all services)	1,160	13.1
Air Force and Marine Corps aircraft	1,220	28.0
Navy aircraft	770	21.4
Combat service and support aircraft (all services)	1,030	10.7
Major warships and submarines	30	19.1
Other ships (auxiliaries and light craft)	115	8.2
Ship conversions	14	3.1
Tactical missiles and torpedoes (all services)	220,400	28.7
Airlift aircraft	14	2.4
Sealift ships	18	5.1
U.S. share of NATO barrier (Army)	. . .	0.9
National intelligence and communications		
Global positioning satellite	12	4.6
Defense meteorological support program	4	1.4
Fleet satellite communications system	9	3.5
Military strategic and tactical relay system	7	8.6
Classified	. . .	8.8
Summary		
Strategic nuclear forces	. . .	31.7
Tactical nuclear forces	. . .	2.5
Conventional forces	. . .	156.6
National intelligence and communications	. . .	26.9
Total	. . .	217.7

Sources: Data from Congressional Budget Office, April 17, 1989; table 16; and author's estimates.

Table 19. U.S. National Defense Outlays, Fiscal Years 1990–94
Billions of 1990 dollars

	Cheney,	Reduced outlays[a]			
Appropriation title	1990	1991	1992	1993	1994
Military personnel	80.4	78.9	77.4	75.9	74.4
Operation and maintenance	91.5	88.5	85.4	82.3	79.2
Procurement	80.0	77.6	75.1	72.6	70.0
Research, development, test, and evaluation	40.0	38.7	37.4	36.1	34.7
Military construction	4.9	4.7	4.5	4.3	4.1
Family housing	3.2	3.1	2.8	2.8	2.5
Revolving and management funds	. . .	0.0	0.1	0.0	0.1
Total	300.0	291.5	282.7	274.1	265.0

Source: Author's estimates.
a. Reductions based on efficiency and arms control prospects. For details, see tables 7, 11, and 15.

Table 20. Status of the Strategic Arms Reduction Talks, June 1989

Agreed Limits

General

  1,600 strategic offensive delivery systems

  6,000 "accountable" warheads on delivery systems

ICBMs and SLBMs[a]

  50 percent reduction in missile throw-weight from Soviet levels

  4,900 warheads on ballistic missiles

  1,540 warheads on 154 Soviet SS-18 ICBMs

Heavy bombers

  16 (or fewer) short-range attack missiles and gravity bombs count as 1 warhead per bomber

  1 long-range ALCM counts as 1 warhead up to some total of ALCMs per bomber[b]

Verification

  Weapons data exchange

  On-site inspections

  Ban on encoding flight-test data

Implementation

  Seven years allowed for cut in ballistic missile warheads to 4,900

  Intermediate reduction: (a) to equal levels (U.S.) or (b) of equal proportions (USSR)

Proposed Limits

3,000–3,300 ceiling on ICBM warheads (U.S.)

800 launchers and 1,600 warheads on mobile ICBMs (USSR)[c]

400 nuclear and 600 non-nuclear sea-launched cruise missiles, or 1,000 total SLCMS (USSR)

1,100 total weapons on heavy bombers (USSR)

Sources: *Washington Post*, June 13, 1989, p. A22; and *New York Times*, June 19, 1989, p. A11.

  a. ICBMs are defined as having a minimum range of 3,300 statute miles; the minimum range for submarine-launched ballistic missiles (SLBMs) is not available.

  b. The United States proposes that no more than 10 air-launched cruise missiles (ALCMs) be counted per bomber regardless of the maximum capacity of the bomber; the USSR defines the total per bomber as the maximum capacity of the bomber. The USSR proposes to count all ALCMs with a range of more than 373 miles; the United States puts the minimum range at 932 miles.

  c. The United States proposed to ban all mobile ICBMs unless verification problems can be solved, but that position has now been changed.

Table 21. Warsaw Pact Data on Armed Forces in Europe, January 30, 1989
Personnel in thousands

Item	Warsaw Pact	NATO
Total armed forces in Europe (personnel)	3,235.1	2,975.2
Total ground forces in Europe (personnel)	1,823.5	2,115.5
Land-based strike aircraft	2,091	2,445
Air defense aviation[a]	5,093	3,055
Combat helicopters[b]	2,785	5,270
Tactical missile launchers	1,608	138
Tanks	59,470	30,690
Antitank missile complexes	11,465	18,070
Infantry combat vehicles and armored transports	70,330	46,900
Artillery[c]	71,560	57,060
Armored-vehicle-launched bridges[d]	2,550	614
Air defense systems[d]	24,400	11,079

Sources: *Arms Control Reporter, 1989* (Institute for Defense and Disarmament Studies), pp. 407.E.1–6; U.S. Arms Control and Disarmament Agency, *Arms Control Update*, no. 10 (December 1988), pp. 4–5; and *New York Times*, May 30, 1989, p. A12.

a. Includes aircraft incapable of operating against ground targets. The Warsaw Pact claims that it deploys 1,829 of these, while NATO deploys only 50.

b. Includes naval helicopters.

c. Consists of rocket-propelled salvo-fire systems, field artillery (75 mm and above), and mortars (50 mm and above).

d. Not provided in Warsaw Pact data. See *Arms Control Update*, no. 10, pp. 4–5, for NATO estimates.

Table 22. NATO-Proposed Conventional Limits from the Atlantic to the Urals[a]

Force	Area I[b]	Area II	Area III	Area IV
NATO	Belgium	Belgium	Belgium	Belgium
	Denmark	Denmark	Denmark	. . .
	France	France	France	. . .
	Greece	. . .	. . .	. . .
	Iceland	. . .	. . .	. . .
	Italy	Italy	Italy	. . .
	Luxembourg	Luxembourg	Luxembourg	Luxembourg
	Netherlands	Netherlands	Netherlands	Netherlands
	Norway	. . .	. . .	. . .
	Portugal	Portugal	. . .	. . .
	Spain	Spain	. . .	. . .
	Turkey	. . .	. . .	. . .
	United Kingdom	United Kingdom	United Kingdom	. . .
	West Germany	West Germany	West Germany	West Germany
Warsaw Pact	Bulgaria	. . .	. . .	. . .
	Czechoslovakia	Czechoslovakia	Czechoslovakia	Czechoslovakia
	East Germany	East Germany	East Germany	East Germany
	Hungary	Hungary	Hungary	. . .
	Poland	Poland	Poland	Poland
	Romania	. . .	. . .	. . .
Soviet military district	Baltic	Baltic	Baltic	. . .
	Byelorussia	Byelorussia	Byelorussia	. . .
	Carpathia	Carpathia	Carpathia	. . .
	Moscow	Moscow	. . .	. . .
	Volga	Volga	. . .	. . .
	Urals	Urals	. . .	. . .
	Leningrad	. . .	. . .	. . .
	Odessa	. . .	. . .	. . .
	Kiev	. . .	. . .	. . .
	Trans-Caucasus	. . .	. . .	. . .
	North Caucasus	. . .	. . .	. . .

Allowable weapons[c]	Area I	Area II	Area III	Area IV
NATO				
Main battle tanks	20,000	11,300	10,300	8,000
Artillery	16,500	9,000	7,600	4,500
Armored troop carriers	28,000	20,000	18,000	11,000
Warsaw Pact				
Main battle tanks	20,000	11,300	10,300	8,000
Artillery	16,500	9,000	7,600	4,500
Armored troop carriers	28,000	20,000	18,000	11,000

Source: U.S. Arms Control and Disarmament Agency, *Arms Control Update*, no. 12 (March 1989), p. 5.

a. According to NATO objectives, in the areas specified, neither NATO nor the Warsaw Pact shall exceed the levels of weapons indicated.

b. This area constitutes NATO's definition of the Atlantic to the Urals.

c. NATO formulated these limits before President Bush, in his proposal of May 28, 1989, indicated a willingness to include military personnel and combat aircraft in the category of allowable weapons. On July 13 NATO therefore proposed that each alliance be limited to 5,700 combat aircraft and 1,900 combat helicopters in the Atlantic-to-the-Urals area, and that no one country be allowed to retain more than 1,700 combat aircraft and 342 combat helicopters, or 30 percent of an alliance total, in the area. For further details, see *Arms Control Reporter, 1989*, pp. 407.E. 30–31.

Table 23. Warsaw Pact Definition of Conventional Limits from the Atlantic to the Urals[a]

Force	ATTU	Central Europe	Zone of contact	Rear zone	Stationed forces[b]	Single country
NATO	Belgium	Belgium	Belgium	...	...	...
	Denmark	Denmark	Denmark	...	...	...
	France	...	...	France	...	...
	Greece	...	Greece	...	...	...
	Iceland	...	...	Iceland	...	...
	Italy	...	Italy	...	...	...
	Luxembourg	Luxembourg	Luxembourg	...	...	...
	Netherlands	Netherlands	Netherlands	...	...	...
	Norway	...	Norway	...	...	...
	Portugal	...	...	Portugal	...	...
	Spain	...	...	Spain	...	...
	Turkey	...	Turkey	...	...	...
	United Kingdom	...	...	United Kingdom	...	...
	West Germany	West Germany	West Germany	...	...	...
Warsaw Pact	Bulgaria	...	Bulgaria	...	...	...
	Czechoslovakia	Czechoslovakia	Czechoslovakia	...	...	...
	East Germany	East Germany	East Germany	...	...	...
	Hungary	Hungary	Hungary	...	...	...
	Poland	Poland	Poland	...	...	...
	Romania	...	Romania	...	...	...

Soviet military district		ATTU		Central Europe		Zone of contact		Rear zone		Stationed forces		Single country	
Baltic		...		Baltic									
Byelorussia		...		Byelorussia									
Carpathia		...		Carpathia									
Moscow		...		Moscow									
Volga		...		Volga									
Urals		...		Urals									
Leningrad		...				Leningrad							
Odessa		...				Odessa							
Kiev		...						Kiev					
Trans-Caucasus		...				Trans-Caucasus							
North Caucasus		...				North Caucasus							

Allowable weapons and troops[c]	ATTU		Central Europe		Zone of contact		Rear zone		Stationed forces		Single country	
	NATO	Pact	NATO	Pact	NATO	Pact	NATO	Pact	NATO	Pact	NATO	Pact
Tanks	20,000	20,000	8,700	8,700	16,000	16,000	4,000	4,000	4,500	4,500	14,000	14,000
Armored personnel carriers	28,000	28,000	14,500	14,500	20,500	20,500	7,500	7,500	7,500	7,500	18,000	18,000
Artillery	24,000	24,000	7,600	7,600	16,500	16,500	7,500	7,500	4,000	4,000	17,000	17,000
Strike aircraft	1,500	1,500	420	420	1,000	1,000	400	400	350	350	1,200	1,200
Helicopters	1,700	1,700	800	800	1,300	1,300	400	400	600	600	1,200	1,200
Troops (thousands)	1,350	1,350	570	570	1,000	1,000	350	350	350	350	920	920

Source: *Arms Control Reporter, 1989*, pp. 407. B. 171–172.

a. The only zone that corresponds to the NATO definition of areas is the ATTU (Atlantic-to-the-Urals) zone. See table 22.
b. The Warsaw Pact refers to these as foreign deployments.
c. Although the two sides appear to agree on the ceiling for tanks and armored personnel carriers in the ATTU area, each defines differently what should be counted in these categories.

Table 24. Official U.S. View of the Conventional Balance in Central Europe, 1987

Capability	Ratio of Warsaw Pact to NATO capabilities		
	1965	1970	1987
Main battle tanks	n.a.	n.a.	>2:1
Combat aircraft	n.a.	n.a.	~2:1
Artillery	n.a.	n.a.	>3:1
Surface-to-air missiles	n.a.	n.a.	~2:1
Combat helicopters	n.a.	n.a.	~2:1
Infantry fighting vehicles	n.a.	n.a.	~3:1
Combat power[a]			
Ground forces	1.5:1	1.9:1	>2.2:1
Tactical air forces	<1.5:1	n.a.	~1.7:1

Source: *Department of Defense Annual Report, Fiscal Year 1988*, pp. 29–30.

n.a. Not available.

a. A measure of lethality of the forces. A ground-force ratio of better than 2:1 in favor of the Warsaw Pact was deemed to give the attacker a decisive advantage over NATO's defenses.

Table 25. NATO and Warsaw Pact Ground and Fighter-Attack Forces in Fiscal 1990 and after Two Stages of Conventional Forces in Europe Reductions

Force and country	*1990*		*CFE (stage 1)*		*CFE (stage 2)*	
	Divisions	*Fighter-attack aircraft*	*Divisions*	*Fighter-attack aircraft*	*Divisions*	*Fighter-attack aircraft*
NATO						
Belgium	3⅓	90	3⅓	74	2⅔	73
Britain	6	228	6	188	4⅔	185
Canada	⅔	42	⅔	35	⅔	34
Denmark	1⅔	60	1⅔	60	1⅔	60
France	10	255	10	211	8⅔	208
Netherlands	3⅓	90	3⅓	74	2⅔	73
United States	6⅑	612	6⅑	528	3⅔	312
West Germany	14⅓	330	14⅓	330	14⅓	330
Total	45.4	1,707	45.4	1,500	39	1,275
Warsaw Pact						
Soviet Union in						
Czechoslovakia	5	150	2	126	1⅓	107
East Germany	19	150	9	126	8	107
Poland	2	150	2	126	1	107
Three Western military districts	34	450	10	379	8⅓	322
Moscow, Volga, Ural districts	19	450	6⅓	379	6⅓	322
Non-Soviet						
Czechoslovakia	10	143	3	121	2⅔	103
East Germany	6	143	2	121	1⅓	103
Poland	15	144	5	122	4⅓	104
Total	110	1,780	39⅓	1,500	33⅓	1,275

Sources: John M. Collins, *U.S./Soviet Military Balance* (Congressional Research Service, August 27, 1984), p. 125; and author's estimates.

Table 26. U.S. Conventional Forces, Selected Fiscal Years, 1990–99

Forces	1990	1994	1997	1999 Case A	1999 Case D
Army divisions					
Active duty[a]	19	18	15⅔	9	7
Reserve	10	10	10	10	10
Marine divisions					
Active duty	3	3	3	3	3
Reserve	1	1	1	1	1
Marine air wings					
Active duty (wings/aircraft)	3/351	3/351	3/351	3/351	3/351
Reserve (wings/aircraft)	1/90	. . .	. . .	. . .	. . .
Air Force fighter-attack wings					
Active duty (wings/aircraft)	24/1,728	24/1,728	20⅔/1,488	12/864	12/864
Reserve (wings/aircraft)	12/864	12/864	12/864	12/864	12/864
Navy					
Carrier battle groups (number/ships)	14/266	12/228	12/228	9/171	6/114
Amphibious forces					
Amphibious ships and escorts	101	76	76	51	51
Mine warfare ships	33	25	25	17	17
Auxiliary ships	8	6	6	4	4
Antisubmarine warfare forces					
Submarines	72	72	72	72	36
Surface combatants	90	90	90	30	30
Auxiliary ships	11	11	11	7	7
P-3 aircraft	260	260	260	260	260
Airlift and sealift					
C-5A/B	110	110	110	110	110
C-141	234	234	234	234	234
KC-10	57	57	57	57	57
C-130	434	434	434	434	434
Transports	71	71	71	71	71
Reserve ships	156	156	156	156	156

Sources: *Department of Defense Annual Report, Fiscal Year, 1990*, pp. 232–33; and author's estimates.

a. These are division equivalents. Independent brigades and regiments are counted as well as numbered divisions.

Table 27. U.S. National Defense Outlays for Major Procurement, Selected Fiscal Years, 1990–99
Billions of 1990 dollars

Year	Total major procurement	Strategic nuclear forces	Tactical nuclear forces	Land forces	Tactical air forces	Navy aircraft and ships	Airlift and sealift	Intelligence and communications
1990	46.4	8.4	0.2	8.2	8.4	14.7	1.7	4.8
1991	45.0	7.3	0.4	8.0	8.5	14.2	1.7	4.9
1992	43.6	6.2	0.6	7.9	8.5	13.6	1.5	5.3
1993	42.1	5.3	0.6	7.7	8.4	13.1	1.3	5.7
1994	40.6	4.5	0.7	7.4	8.2	12.4	1.2	6.2
1997	38.5	4.4	0.7	6.9	7.3	12.0	1.2	6.0
1999								
Case A	29.1	3.3	0.6	4.6	5.1	9.5	0.9	5.1
Case B	26.3	3.2	0.3	3.9	4.8	8.4	0.9	4.8
Case C	23.8	3.2	0.3	3.3	4.8	6.6	0.8	4.8
Case D	21.9	3.1	0.3	3.2	4.7	6.3	0.8	3.5

Source: Author's estimates.

Table 28. U.S. National Defense Outlays in Fiscal Years 1997 and 1999
Billions of 1990 dollars

Appropriation title	Reduced 1997[a]	1999[b]			
		Case A	Case B	Case C	Case D
Military personnel	70.7	56.9	55.7	51.6	50.8
Operation and maintenance	74.6	54.8	50.9	45.3	43.5
Procurement	66.3	50.1	45.4	41.1	37.8
Research, development, test, and evaluation	33.5	28.6	28.1	26.9	24.4
Military construction	3.8	2.6	2.5	2.2	1.9
Family housing	2.4	1.9	1.9	1.8	1.7
Revolving and management funds	0.0	0.0	0.0	0.0	0.0
Total	251.3	194.9	184.5	168.9	160.1

Source: Author's estimates.
a. Reductions as a result of a START and CFE treaties. For details, see tables 9, 26, and 27.
b. Reductions as a result of further agreements and reciprocal actions. For details, see tables 9, 26, and 27.

Table 29. U.S. Peacetime Deployment of Conventional Forces, Fiscal Year 1999 (Case D)

Deployment area	Army divisions		Marine Corps, division/wing		Air Force, fighter-attack wings		Navy vessels
	Active	Reserve	Active	Reserve	Active	Reserve	
West Germany	3⅔	…	…	…	7⅓	…	…
Japan (Okinawa)	…	…	1/1	…	…	…	129
Second Fleet (Atlantic)	…	…	…	…	…	…	129
Third Fleet (Pacific)	…	…	…	…	…	…	128
Alaska	⅓	…	…	…	⅔	…	…
Panama	⅓	…	…	…	⅔	…	…
Continental United States	2⅔	10	2/2	1/0	3⅓	12	…
Total	7	10	3/3	1/0	12	12	257

Source: Author's estimates.

Table 30. U.S. Deployment of Conventional Forces by Planning Contingency, Fiscal Year 1999 (Case D)

Contingency area	Army divisions		Marine Corps, division/wing		Air Force, fighter-attack wings		Navy vessels
	Active	Reserve	Active	Reserve	Active	Reserve	
West Germany	3⅔	10	...	...	7⅓	12	...
Atlantic sea-lanes	...	...	...	...	...	...	36
Persian Gulf	1	...	2/2	...	1⅓	...	74
Pacific sea-lanes	...	...	...	...	...	...	35
Latin America	1	...	1/1	1/0	1⅓	...	74
Alaska	⅔	...	...	...	1	...	...
Panama	⅔	...	...	...	1	...	...
Continental United States	...	...	...	...	...	...	38[a]
Total	7	10	3/3	1/0	12	12	257

Source: Author's estimates.
a. Two carrier battle groups in overhaul.

Table 31. U.S. Outlays for the Defense of Europe, Fiscal Years 1990, 1999 (Case D)
Billions of 1990 dollars

Item	1990	1999 (Case D)
Tactical nuclear capabilities	2.0	2.0
Central Europe	74.9	34.8
North Norway	16.1	. . .
Mediterranean	9.1	. . .
Atlantic	23.9	5.3
Total	126.0	42.1
Percent of national defense outlays	42	26.3

Source: Author's estimates based on table 12.

Table 32. Summary of U.S. Forces and Costs, Fiscal Years 1990–99
Outlays in billions of 1990 dollars

| | Cheney, 1990 | | Reduced, 1994 | | START, CFE, 1997 | | 1999 | | | | | | | |
| | | | | | | | Case A | | Case B | | Case C | | Case D | |
Item	Num-ber	Out-lays	Num-ber	Out-lays	Num-ber	Out-lays	Num-ber	Out-lays	Num-ber	Out-lays	Num-ber	Out-lays	Num-ber	Out-lays
Strategic nuclear forces														
Bombers	276	22.7	90	8.4	90	8.4	41	3.7	41	3.7	41	3.7	...	3.6
Air defense	249	1.2	180	0.7	180	0.7	180	0.7	180	0.7	180	0.7	...	0.7
ICBMs	1,000	7.4	342	2.1	289	1.7	100	0.6	100	0.6	100	0.6	...	0.6
SLBMs	608	11.5	528	11.1	472	10.1	408	9.1	408	9.1	408	9.1	...	9.1
Other	...	9.2	...	6.8	...	6.8	...	6.8	...	6.8	...	6.8	...	5.9
Tactical nuclear forces														
Battlefield	2,125	0.2	2,125	0.2	2,125	0.2	2,125	0.2	2,125	0.2	2,125	0.2	2,125	0.2
Interdiction	5,463	1.8	5,463	3.3	5,463	3.3	5,463	3.3	4,705	1.8	4,705	1.8	4,705	1.8
Conventional forces														
Army divisions														
Active	19	64.9	18	61.5	15⅔	53.5	9	30.7	9	30.7	7	23.9	7	23.9
Reserve	10	10.0	10	9.8	10	9.8	10	9.8	10	4.8	10	4.8	10	4.8
Marine divisions														
Active	3	3.8	3	3.8	3	3.8	3	3.8	3	3.8	3	3.8	3	3.8
Reserve	1	0.5	1	0.5	1	0.5	1	0.5	1	0.5	1	0.5	1	0.5
Marine combat aircraft (wings/aircraft)	4/ 441	4.2	3/ 351	4.2	3/ 351	4.2	3/ 351	4.2	3/ 351	4.2	3/ 351	4.2	3/ 351	4.2
Air Force combat aircraft														
Active (wings/aircraft)	24/ 1,728	30.8	24/ 1,728	30.8	20⅔/ 1,488	26.5	12/ 864	15.5	12/ 864	15.5	12/ 864	15.5	12/ 864	15.5
Reserve (wings/aircraft)	12/ 864	5.0	12/ 864	5.0	12/ 864	5.0	12/ 864	5.0	12/ 864	5.0	12/ 864	5.0	12/ 864	5.0

	14/ 266	12/ 288	12/ 228	9/ 171	9/ 171	6/ 114	6/ 114
Navy							
Carrier battle groups (number/ships)	41.1	35.2	35.2	26.4	26.4	17.6	17.6
Amphibious groups							
Amphibious ships and escorts	101 / 6.7	76 / 5.0	76 / 5.0	51 / 3.3	51 / 3.3	51 / 3.3	51 / 3.3
Mine warfare ships	33 / 0.5	25 / 0.4	25 / 0.4	17 / 0.3	17 / 0.3	17 / 0.3	17 / 0.3
Auxiliary ships	8 / 1.2	6 / 0.9	6 / 0.9	4 / 0.6	4 / 0.6	4 / 0.6	4 / 0.6
Antisubmarine warfare							
Attack submarines	72 / 8.4	72 / 8.4	72 / 8.4	72 / 8.4	72 / 8.4	36 / 4.5	36 / 4.5
Surface combatants	90 / 5.7	90 / 5.7	90 / 5.7	30 / 1.9	30 / 1.9	30 / 1.9	30 / 1.9
Auxiliary ships	11 / 2.5	11 / 2.5	11 / 2.5	7 / 1.4	7 / 1.4	7 / 1.4	7 / 1.4
P-3 aircraft	260 / 2.7	260 / 2.7	260 / 2.7	260 / 2.7	260 / 2.7	260 / 2.7	260 / 2.7
Airlift and sealift							
Airlift aircraft	920 / 9.0	920 / 7.0	920 / 7.0	920 / 7.0	920 / 7.0	920 / 7.0	920 / 7.0
Sealift aircraft	222 / 2.0	222 / 2.0	222 / 2.0	222 / 2.0	222 / 2.0	222 / 2.0	222 / 2.0
Intelligence and communications	… / 26.0	… / 26.0	… / 26.0	… / 26.0	… / 26.0	… / 26.0	… / 18.2
Retired pay accrual	… / 21.0	… / 21.0	… / 21.0	… / 21.0	… / 21.0	… / 21.0	… / 21.0
Addenda							
Reduced program[a]							
050 outlays	300.0	265.0	251.3	194.9	184.5	168.9	160.1
050 budget authority	305.0	269.4	255.5	198.2	187.6	171.7	162.8
051 outlays	289.9	256.1	242.9	188.4	178.3	163.2	154.7
051 budget authority	295.6	261.1	247.6	192.0	181.8	166.4	157.7
Cheney[a]							
050 outlays	300.0	318.5	…	…	…	…	…
050 budget authority	305.0	323.8	…	…	…	…	…
051 outlays	289.9	307.8	…	…	…	…	…
051 budget authority	295.6	313.8	…	…	…	…	…

Sources: Author's estimates based on tables 7, 11, 12, and 15.

a. The 050 account, entitled "National Defense," includes the funds for the Department of Defense, the military applications of atomic weapons, and several lesser functions. The 051 account consists of funds for the Department of Defense only.

DATE DUE